THE DEVIL'S

DICTIONARY

BY AMBROSE BIERCE

ILLUSTRATIONS BY JEAN-CLAUDE SUARÈS

THOMAS Y. CROWELL, PUBLISHERS
ESTABLISHED 1834
NEW YORK

THE DEVIL'S DICTIONARY

L.C. # 78-3318
ISBN 0-690-01764-2

ISBN 0-690-01765-0 pbk.

THE DEVIL'S DICTIONARY

A

ABASEMENT, *n.*
A decent and customary mental attitude in the presence of wealth or power. Peculiarly appropriate in an employee when addressing an employer.

ABATIS, *n.*
Rubbish in front of a fort, to prevent the rubbish outside from molesting the rubbish inside.

ABDICATION, *n.*
An act whereby a sovereign attests his sense of the high temperature of the throne.

> Poor Isabella's dead, whose
>   abdication
> Set all tongues wagging in the
>   Spanish nation.
> For that performance 'twere unfair
>   to scold her:
> She wisely left a throne too hot to
>   hold her.
> To History she'll be no royal
>   riddle—
> Merely a plain parched pea that
>   jumped the griddle.
>   *G. J.*

ABDOMEN, *n.*
The temple of the god Stomach, in whose worship, with sacrificial rights, all true men engage. From women this ancient faith commands but a stammering assent. They sometimes minister at the altar in a half-hearted and ineffective way, but true reverence for the one deity that men really adore they know not.

ABILITY, *n.*
The natural equipment to accomplish some small part of the meaner ambitions distinguishing able men from dead ones. In the last analysis ability is commonly found to consist mainly in a high degree of solemnity. Perhaps, however, this impressive quality is rightly appraised; it is no easy task to be solemn.

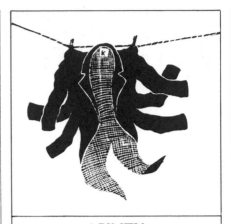

ABILITY

ABNORMAL, *adj.*
Not conforming to standard. In matters of thought and conduct, to be independent is to be abnormal, to be abnormal is to be detested. Wherefore the lexicographer adviseth a striving toward a straiter resemblance to the Average Man than he hath to himself. Whoso attaineth thereto shall have peace, the prospect of death and the hope of Hell.

ABORIGINES, *n.*
Persons of little worth found cumbering the soil of a newly discovered country. They soon cease to cumber; they fertilize.

ABSENTEE, *n.*
A person with an income who has had the forethought to remove himself from the sphere of exaction.

ABSOLUTE, *adj.*
Independent, irresponsible. An absolute monarchy is one in which the sovereign does as he pleases so long as he pleases the assassins. Not many absolute monarchies are left, most of them having been replaced by limited monarchies, where the sovereign's power for evil (and for good) is greatly curtailed, and by republics, which are governed by chance.

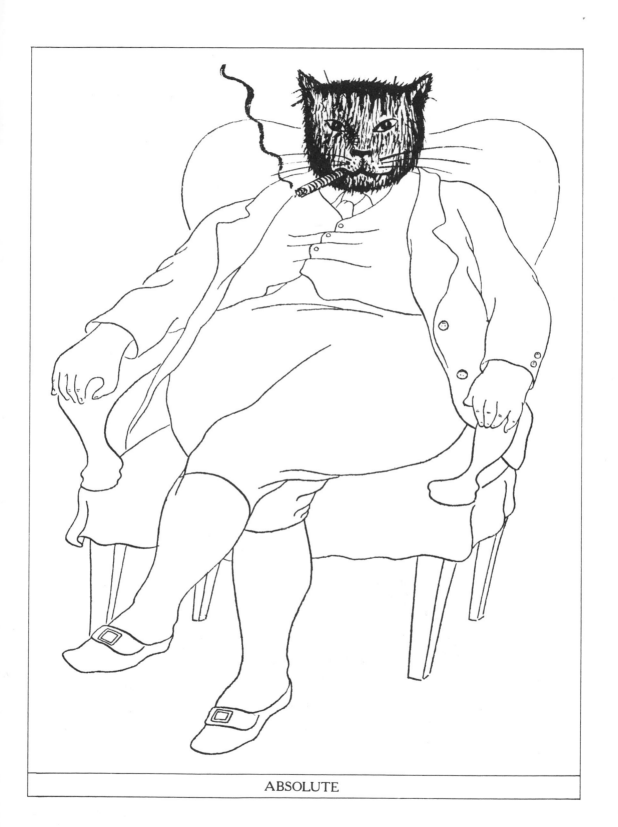

ABSOLUTE

ABSTAINER, *n.*
A weak person who yields to the
temptation of denying himself a
pleasure. A total abstainer is one
who abstains from everything but
abstention, and especially from
inactivity in the affairs of others.

> Said a man to a crapulent youth: "I
>   thought
>   You a total abstainer, my son."
> "So I am, so I am," said the
>   scapegrace caught—
> "But not, sir, a bigoted one."
>
> *G. J.*

ABSURDITY, *n.*
A statement or belief manifestly
inconsistent with one's own opinion.

ACADEME, *n.*
An ancient school where morality
and philosophy were taught.

ACADEMY, *n.*
(from academe). A modern school
where football is taught.

ACCIDENT, *n.*
An inevitable occurrence due to the
action of immutable natural laws.

ACCIDENT

ACCOMPLICE, *n.*
One associated with another in a
crime, having guilty knowledge and
complicity, as an attorney who
defends a criminal, knowing him
guilty. This view of the attorney's
position in the matter has not
hitherto commanded the assent of
attorneys, no one having offered
them a fee for assenting.

ACCORD, *n.*
Harmony.

ACCORDION, *n.*
An instrument in harmony with the
sentiments of an assassin.

ACCOUNTABILITY, *n.*
The mother of caution.

> "My accountability, bear in mind,"
>   Said the Grand Vizier: "Yes, yes,"
> Said the Shah: "I do—'tis the only
>   kind
>   Of ability you possess."
>
> *Joram Tate.*

ACCUSE, *v. t.*
To affirm another's guilt or
unworth; most commonly as a
justification of ourselves for having
wronged him.

ACEPHALOUS, *adj.*
In the surprising condition of the
Crusader who absently pulled at his
forelock some hours after a Saracen
scimitar had, unconsciously to him,
passed through his neck, as related
by de Joinville.

ACHIEVEMENT, *n.*
The death of endeavor and the birth
of disgust.

ACKNOWLEDGE, *v. t.*
To confess. Acknowledgment of one
another's faults is the highest duty
imposed by our love of truth.

ACQUAINTANCE, *n.*
A person whom we know well
enough to borrow from, but not
well enough to lend to. A degree of
friendship called slight when its
object is poor or obscure, and
intimate when he is rich or famous.

ACTUALLY, *adv.*
Perhaps; possibly.

ADAGE, *n.*
Boned wisdom for weak teeth.

ADAMANT, *n.*
A mineral frequently found beneath
a corset. Soluble in solicitate of
gold.

ADDER, *n.*
A species of snake. So called from
its habit of adding funeral outlays
to the other expenses of living.

ADHERENT, *n.*
A follower who has not yet obtained
all that he expects to get.

ADMINISTRATION, *n.*
An ingenious abstraction in politics,
designed to receive the kicks and
cuffs due to the premier or
president. A man of straw, proof
against bad-egging and deadcatting.

ADMIRAL, *n.*
That part of a war-ship which does
the talking while the figure-head
does the thinking.

ADMIRATION, *n.*
Our polite recognition of another's
resemblance to ourselves.

ADMONITION, *n.*
Gentle reproof, as with a meat-axe.
Friendly warning.

> Consigned, by way of admonition,
> His soul forever to perdition.
>
> *Jubibras.*

ADORE

ADORE, *v. t.*
To venerate expectantly.

ADVICE, *n.*
The smallest current coin.

> "The man was in such deep
>   distress,"
> Said Tom, "that I could do no less
> Than give him good advice." Said
>   Jim:
> "If less could have been done for him
> I know you well enough, my son,
> To know that's what you would have
>   done."
>
> *Jebel Jocordy.*

AFFIANCED, *pp.*
Fitted with an ankle-ring for the
ball-and-chain.

AFRICAN, *n.*
A nigger that votes our way.

AGE, *n.*
That period of life in which we
compound for the vices that we still
cherish by reviling those that we
have no longer the enterprise to
commit.

AGITATOR, *n.*
A statesman who shakes the fruit
trees of his neighbors—to dislodge
the worms.

AIM, *n.*
The task we set our wishes to.

> "Cheer up! Have you no aim in life?"
>   She tenderly inquired.
> "An aim? Well, no, I haven't, wife:
>   The fact is—I have fired."
>
> > *G. J.*

AIR, *n.*
A nutritious substance supplied by a bountiful Providence for the fattening of the poor.

ALDERMAN, *n.*
An ingenious criminal who covers his secret thieving with a pretence of open marauding.

ALIEN, *n.*
An American sovereign in his probationary state.

ALLAH, *n.*
The Mahometan Supreme Being, as distinguished from the Christian, Jewish, and so forth.

> Allah's good laws I faithfully have
>   kept,
> And ever for the sins of man have
>   wept;
>   And sometimes kneeling in the
>   temple I
> Have reverently crossed my hands
>   and slept.
>
> > *Junker Barlow.*

ALLEGIANCE, *n.*

> This thing Allegiance, as I suppose,
> Is a ring fitted in the subject's nose,
> Whereby that organ is kept rightly
>   pointed
> To smell the sweetness of the Lord's
>   anointed.
>
> > *G. J.*

ALLIANCE, *n.*
In international politics, the union of two thieves who have their hands so deeply inserted in each other's pocket that they cannot separately plunder a third.

ALLIGATOR

ALLIGATOR, *n.*
The crocodile of America, superior in every detail to the crocodile of the effete monarchies of the Old World. Herodotus says the Indus is, with one exception, the only river that produces crocodiles, but they appear to have gone West and grown up with the other rivers. From the notches on his back the alligator is called a sawrian.

ALONE, *adj.*
In bad company.

AMBIDEXTROUS, *adj.*
Able to pick with equal skill a right-hand pocket or a left.

AMBITION, *n.*
An overmastering desire to be vilified by enemies while living and made ridiculous by friends when dead.

AMNESTY, *n.*
The state's magnanimity to those offenders whom it would be too expensive to punish.

ANOINT, *v. t.*
To grease a king or other great functionary already sufficiently slippery.

ANOINT

ANTIPATHY, *n.*
The sentiment inspired by one's
friend's friend.

APHORISM, *n.*
Predigested wisdom.

> The flabby wine-skin of his brain
> Yields to some pathologic strain,
> And voids from its unstored abysm
> The driblet of an aphorism.
> *"The Mad Philosopher,"* 1697.

APOLOGIZE, *v. i.*
To lay the foundation for a future
offence.

APOSTATE, *n.*
A leech who, having penetrated the
shell of a turtle only to find that the
creature has long been dead, deems
it expedient to form a new
attachment to a fresh turtle.

APOTHECARY, *n.*
The physician's accomplice,
undertaker's benefactor and grave
worm's provider.

> When Jove sent blessings to all men
> that are,
> And Mercury conveyed them in a
> jar,
> That friend of tricksters introduced
> by stealth
> Disease for the apothecary's health,
> Whose gratitude impelled him to
> proclaim:
> "My deadliest drug shall bear my
> patron's name!"
> *G. J.*

APPEAL, *v. t.*
In law, to put the dice into the box
for another throw.

APPETITE, *n.*
An instinct thoughtfully implanted
by Providence as a solution to the
labor question.

APPLAUSE, *n.*
The echo of a platitude.

APRIL FOOL

APRIL FOOL, *n.*
The March fool with another month
added to his folly.

ARCHBISHOP, *n.*
An ecclesiastical dignitary one
point holier than a bishop.

> If I were a jolly archbishop,
> On Fridays I'd eat all the fish up—
> Salmon and flounders and smelts;
> On other days everything else.
> *Jodo Rem.*

ARCHITECT, *n.*
One who drafts a plan of your
house, and plans a draft of your
money.

ARDOR, *n.*
The quality that distinguishes love
without knowledge.

ARENA, *n.*
In politics, an imaginary rat-pit in
which the statesman wrestles with
his record.

ARISTOCRACY, *n.*
Government by the best men. (In
this sense the word is obsolete; so is
that kind of government.) Fellows
that wear downy hats and clean
shirts—guilty of education and
suspected of bank accounts.

ARMOR, *n.*
The kind of clothing worn by a man
whose tailor is a blacksmith.

ARRAYED, *pp.*
Drawn up and given an orderly
disposition, as a rioter hanged to a
lamppost.

ARREST, *v. t.*
Formally to detain one accused of
unusualness.

> God made the world in six days
> and was arrested on the seventh.
> — *The Unauthorized Version.*

ARSENIC, *n.*
A kind of cosmetic greatly affected
by the ladies, whom it greatly
affects in turn.

> "Eat arsenic? Yes, all you get,"
> Consenting, he did speak up:
> " 'Tis better you should eat it, pet,
> Than put it in my teacup."
> *Joel Huck.*

ART, *n.*
This word has no definition. Its
origin is related as follows by the
ingenious Father Gassalasca Jape,
S.J.

> One day a wag—what would the
>   wretch be at?—
> Shifted a letter of the cipher RAT,
> And said it was a god's name!
>   Straight arose
> Fantastic priests and postulants
>   (with shows,
> And mysteries, and mummeries, and
>   hymns,
> And disputations dire that lamed
>   their limbs)
> To serve his temple and maintain
>   the fires,
> Expound the law, manipulate the
>   wires.

> Amazed, the populace the rites
>   attend,
> Believe whate'er they cannot
>   comprehend,
> And, inly edified to learn that two
> Half-hairs joined so and so (as Art
>   can do)
> Have sweeter values and a grace
>   more fit
> Than Nature's hairs that never have
>   been split,
> Bring cates and wines for sacrificial
>   feasts,
> And sell their garments to support
>   the priests.

ARTLESSNESS, *n.*
A certain engaging quality to
which women attain by long study
and severe practice upon the
admiring male, who is pleased to
fancy it resembles the candid
simplicity of his young.

ASS, *n.*
A public singer with a good voice
but no ear. In Virginia City,
Nevada, he is called the Washoe
Canary, in Dakota, the Senator, and
everywhere the Donkey. The animal
is widely and variously celebrated
in the literature, art and religion of
every age and country; no other so
engages and fires the human
imagination as this noble
vertebrate. Indeed, it is doubted by
some (Ramasilus, *lib. II., De Clem.,*
and C. Stantatus, *De
Temperamente*) if it is not a god;
and as such we know it was
worshiped by the Etruscans, and, if
we may believe Macrobious, by the
Cupasians also. Of the only two
animals admitted into the
Mahometan Paradise along with
the souls of men, the ass that
carried Balaam is one, the dog of
the Seven Sleepers the other. This
is no small distinction. From what
has been written about this beast
might be compiled a library of
great splendor and magnitude,
rivaling that of the Shakespearean
cult, and that which clusters about
the Bible. It may be said, generally,
that all literature is more or less
Asinine.

B

BAAL, *n.*
An old deity formerly much worshiped under various names. As Baal he was popular with the Phoenicians; as Belus or Bel he had the honor to be served by the priest Berosus, who wrote the famous account of the Deluge; as Babel he had a tower partly erected to his glory on the Plain of Shinar. From Babel comes our English word "babble." Under whatever name worshiped, Baal is the Sun-god. As Beelzebub he is the god of flies, which are begotten of the sun's rays on stagnant water. In Physicia Baal is still worshiped as Bolus, and as Belly he is adored and served with abundant sacrifice by the priests of Guttledom.

BABE or **BABY**, *n.*
A misshapen creature of no particular age, sex, or condition, chiefly remarkable for the violence of the sympathies and antipathies it excites in others, itself without sentiment or emotion. There have been famous babes; for example, little Moses, from whose adventure in the bulrushes the Egyptian hierophants of seven centuries before doubtless derived their idle tale of the child Osiris being preserved on a floating lotus leaf.

BACCHUS, *n.*
A convenient deity invented by the ancients as an excuse for getting drunk.

> Is public worship, then, a sin,
> That for devotions paid to Bacchus
> The lictors dare to run us in,
> And resolutely thump and whack us?
>
> *Jorace.*

BACK, *n.*
That part of your friend which it is your privilege to contemplate in your adversity.

BACKBITE, *v. t.*
To speak of a man as you find him when he can't find you.

BAIT, *n.*
A preparation that renders the hook more palatable. The best kind is beauty.

BAPTISM, *n.*
A sacred rite of such efficacy that he who finds himself in heaven without having undergone it will be unhappy forever. It is performed with water in two ways—by immersion, or plunging, and by aspersion, or sprinkling.

BAPTISM

BAROMETER, *n.*
An ingenious instrument which
indicates what kind of weather we
are having.

BARRACK, *n.*
A house in which soldiers enjoy a
portion of that of which it is their
business to deprive others.

BASTINADO, *n.*
The act of walking on wood without
exertion.

BATH, *n.*
A kind of mystic ceremony
substituted for religious worship,
with what spiritual efficacy has not
been determined.

> The man who taketh a steam bath
> He loseth all the skin he hath,
> And, for he's boiled a brilliant red,
> Thinketh to cleanliness he's wed,
> Forgetting that his lungs he's soiling
> With dirty vapors of the boiling.
> *Richard Gwow.*

BATTLE, *n.*
A method of untying with the teeth
a political knot that would not yield
to the tongue.

BEARD, *n.*
The hair that is commonly cut off
by those who justly execrate the
absurd Chinese custom of shaving
the head.

BEAUTY, *n.*
The power by which a woman
charms a lover and terrifies a
husband.

BEFRIEND, *v. t.*
To make an ingrate.

BEG, *v.*
To ask for something with an
earnestness proportioned to the
belief that it will not be given.

BEGGAR, *n.*
One who has relied on the
assistance of his friends.

BEHAVIOR, *n.*
Conduct, as determined, not by
principle, but by breeding. The
word seems to be somewhat loosely
used in Dr. Jamrach Holobom's
translation of the following lines in
the *Dies Irae:*

> Recordare, Jesu pie,
> Quod sum causa tuae viae.
> Ne me perdas illa die.

> Pray remember, sacred Savior,
> Whose the thoughtless hand that
>   gave your
> Death-blow. Pardon such behavior.

BENEFACTOR, *n.*
One who makes heavy purchases of
ingratitude, without, however,
materially affecting the price,
which is still within the means of
all.

BENEFACTOR

BIGAMY, *n.*
A mistake in taste for which the
wisdom of the future will adjudge a
punishment called trigamy.

BIGOT, *n.*
One who is obstinately and
zealously attached to an opinion
that you do not entertain.

BIRTH

BIRTH, *n.*
The first and direst of all disasters.
As to the nature of it there appears
to be no uniformity. Castor and
Pollux were born from the egg.
Pallas came out of a skull. Galatea
was once a block of stone. Peresilis,
who wrote in the tenth century,
avers that he grew up out of the
ground where a priest had spilled
holy water. It is known that
Arimaxus was derived from a hole
in the earth, made by a stroke of
lightning. Leucomedon was the son
of a cavern in Mount Aetna, and I
have myself seen a man come out of
a wine cellar.

BLANK-VERSE, *n.*
Unrhymed iambic pentameters—
the most difficult kind of English
verse to write acceptably; a kind,
therefore, much affected by those
who cannot acceptably write any
kind.

BODY-SNATCHER, *n.*
A robber of grave-worms. One who
supplies the young physicians with
that with which the old physicians
have supplied the undertaker. The
hyena.

BONDSMAN, *n.*
A fool who, having property of his
own, undertakes to become
responsible for that entrusted by
another to a third.
    Philippe of Orleans wishing to
appoint one of his favorites, a
dissolute nobleman, to a high
office, asked him what security he
would be able to give. "I need no
bondsmen," he replied, "for I can
give you my word of honor." "And
pray what may be the value of
that?" inquired the amused
Regent. "Monsieur, it is worth its
weight in gold."

BORE, *n.*
A person who talks when you wish
him to listen.

BOTANY, *n.*
The science of vegetables—those
that are not good to eat, as well as
those that are. It deals largely with
their flowers, which are commonly
badly designed, inartistic in color,
and ill-smelling.

BOTTLE-NOSED, *adj.*
Having a nose created in the image
of its maker.

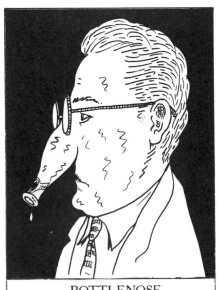

BOTTLENOSE

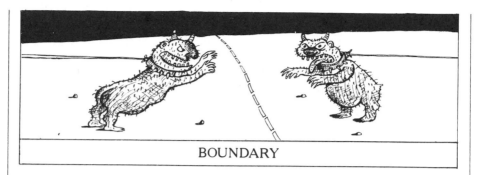

BOUNDARY

BOUNDARY, *n.*
In political geography, an imaginary line between two nations, separating the imaginary rights of one from the imaginary rights of the other.

BOUNTY, *n.*
The liberality of one who has much, in permitting one who has nothing to get all that he can.

A single swallow, it is said, devours ten millions of insects every year. The supplying of these insects I take to be a signal instance of the Creator's bounty in providing for the lives of His creatures. — *Henry Ward Beecher.*

BRAHMA, *n.*
He who created the Hindoos, who are preserved by Vishnu and destroyed by Siva — a rather neater division of labor than is found among the deities of some other nations. The Abracadabranese, for example, are created by Sin, maintained by Theft and destroyed by Folly. The priests of Brahma, like those of the Abracadabranese, are holy and learned men who are never naughty.

O Brahma, thou rare old Divinity,
First Person of the Hindoo Trinity,
You sit there so calm and securely,
With feet folded up so demurely —
You're the First Person Singular,
    surely.

       Polydore Smith.

BRAIN, *n.*
An apparatus with which we think that we think. That which distinguishes the man who is content to *be* something from the man who wishes to *do* something. A man of great wealth, or one who has been pitchforked into high station, has commonly such a headful of brain that his neighbors cannot keep their hats on. In our civilization, and under our republican form of government, brain is so highly honored that it is rewarded by exemption from the cares of office.

BRIDE, *n.*
A woman with a fine prospect of happiness behind her.

BRIDE

BRUTE, *n.*
See HUSBAND.

C

CAABA, *n.*
A large stone presented by the archangel Gabriel to the patriarch Abraham, and preserved at Mecca. The patriarch had perhaps asked the archangel for bread.

CABBAGE, *n.*
A familiar kitchen-garden vegetable about as large and wise as a man's head.

The cabbage is so called from Cabagius, a prince who on ascending the throne issued a decree appointing a High Council of Empire consisting of the members of his predecessor's Ministry and the cabbages in the royal garden. When any of his Majesty's measures of state policy miscarried conspicuously it was gravely announced that several members of the High Council had been beheaded, and his murmuring subjects were appeased.

CALAMITY, *n.*
A more than commonly plain and unmistakable reminder that the affairs of this life are not of our own ordering. Calamities are of two kinds: misfortune to ourselves, and good fortune to others.

CALAMITY

CALLOUS, *adj.*
Gifted with great fortitude to bear the evils afflicting another.

When Zeno was told that one of his enemies was no more he was observed to be deeply moved. "What!" said one of his disciples, "you weep at the death of an enemy?" "Ah, 'tis true," replied the great Stoic; "but you should see me smile at the death of a friend."

CALUMNUS, *n.*
A graduate of the School for Scandal.

CAMEL, *n.*
A quadruped (the *Splaypes humpidorsus)* of great value to the show business. There are two kinds of camels—the camel proper and the camel improper. It is the latter that is always exhibited.

CANNIBAL, *n.*
A gastronome of the old school who preserves the simple tastes and adheres to the natural diet of the pre-pork period.

CANNON, *n.*
An instrument employed in the rectification of national boundaries.

CANONICALS, *n.*
The motley worn by Jesters of the Court of Heaven.

CAPITAL, *n.*
The seat of misgovernment. That which provides the fire, the pot, the dinner, the table and the knife and fork for the anarchist; the part of the repast that himself supplies is the disgrace before meat. *Capital Punishment,* a penalty regarding the justice and expediency of which many worthy persons—including all the assassins—entertain grave misgivings.

CANNIBAL

CAT, *n.*
A soft, indestructible automaton
provided by nature to be kicked
when things go wrong in the
domestic circle.

CAT

This is a dog,
    This is a cat,
This is a frog,
    This is a rat.
Run, dog, mew, cat,
Jump, frog, gnaw, rat.
                        Elevenson.

CAVILER, *n.*
A critic of our own work.

CEMETERY, *n.*
An isolated suburban spot where
mourners match lies, poets write at
a target and stonecutters spell for a
wager. The inscriptions following
will serve to illustrate the success
attained in these Olympian games:

His virtues were so conspicuous that
his enemies, unable to overlook them,
denied them, and his friends, to whose
loose lives they were a rebuke,
represented them as vices. They are here
commemorated by his family, who
shared them.

In the earth we here prepare a
Place to lay our little Clara.
    —*Thomas M. and Mary Frazer.*

P.S.—Gabriel will raise her.

CHILDHOOD, *n.*
The period of human life
intermediate between the idiocy of
infancy and the folly of youth—two
removes from the sin of manhood
and three from the remorse of age.

CHRISTIAN, *n.*
One who believes that the New
Testament is a divinely inspired
book admirably suited to the
spiritual needs of his neighbor. One
who follows the teachings of Christ
in so far as they are not inconsistent
with a life of sin.

CIRCUS, *n.*
A place where horses, ponies and
elephants are permitted to see men,
women and children acting the fool.

CLAIRVOYANT, *n.*
A person, commonly a woman, who
has the power of seeing that which
is invisible to her patron—namely,
that he is a blockhead.

CLARIONET, *n.*
An instrument of torture operated
by a person with cotton in his ears.
There are two instruments that are
worse than a clarionet—two
clarionets.

CLERGYMAN, *n.*
A man who undertakes the
management of our spiritual affairs
as a method of bettering his
temporal ones.

CLIO, *n.*
One of the nine Muses. Clio's
function was to preside over
history—which she did with great
dignity, many of the prominent
citizens of Athens occupying seats
on the platform, the meetings being
addressed by Messrs. Xenophon,
Herodotus and other popular
speakers.

CLOCK

CLOCK, *n.*
A machine of great moral value to man, allaying his concern for the future by reminding him what a lot of time remains to him.

> A busy man complained one day:
> "I get no time!" "What's that you
>   say?"
> Cried out his friend, a lazy quiz;
> "You have, sir, all the time there is.
> There's plenty, too, and don't you
>   doubt it—
> We're never for an hour without it."
> *Purzil Crofe.*

COMFORT, *n.*
A state of mind produced by contemplation of a neighbor's uneasiness.

COMMENDATION, *n.*
The tribute that we pay to achievements that resemble, but do not equal, our own.

COMMERCE, *n.*
A kind of transaction in which A plunders from B the goods of C, and for compensation B picks the pocket of D of money belonging to E.

COMPROMISE, *n.*
Such an adjustment of conflicting interests as gives each adversary the satisfaction of thinking he has got what he ought not to have, and is deprived of nothing except what was justly his due.

COMPULSION, *n.*
The eloquence of power.

CONDOLE, *v. i.*
To show that bereavement is a smaller evil than sympathy.

CONFIDANT, CONFIDANTE, *n.*
One entrusted by A with the secrets of B, confided by *him* to C.

CONGRATULATION, *n.*
The civility of envy.

CONGRESS, *n.*
A body of men who meet to repeal laws.

CONNOISSEUR, *n.*
A specialist who knows everything about something and nothing about anything else.

An old wine-bibber having been smashed in a railway collision, some wine was poured upon his lips to revive him. "Pauillac, 1873," he murmured and died.

CONSERVATIVE, *n.*
A statesman who is enamored of existing evils, as distinguished from the Liberal, who wishes to replace them with others.

CONSOLATION, *n.*
The knowledge that a better man is more unfortunate than yourself.

CONSUL, *n.*
In American politics, a person who having failed to secure an office from the people is given one by the Administration on condition that he leave the country.

CONSULT, *v. t.*
To seek another's approval of a course already decided on.

CONTEMPT, *n.*
The feeling of a prudent man for an enemy who is too formidable safely to be opposed.

CONTROVERSY, *n.*
A battle in which spittle or ink replaces the injurious cannon-ball and the inconsiderate bayonet.

CONVENT, *n.*
A place of retirement for women who wish for leisure to meditate upon the vice of idleness.

CONVERSATION, *n.*
A fair for the display of the minor mental commodities, each exhibitor being too intent upon the arrangement of his own wares to observe those of his neighbor.

CORONATION, *n.*
The ceremony of investing a sovereign with the outward and visible signs of his divine right to be blown skyhigh with a dynamite bomb.

CORPORAL, *n.*
A man who occupies the lowest rung of the military ladder.

> Fiercely the battle raged and, sad to
>   tell,
> Our corporal heroically fell!
> Fame from her height looked down
>   upon the brawl
> And said: "He hadn't very far to fall."
> *Giacomo Smith.*

CORPORATION, *n.*
An ingenious device for obtaining individual profit without individual responsibility.

CORSAIR, *n.*
A politician of the seas.

COURT FOOL, *n.*
The plaintiff.

COWARD, *n.*
One who in a perilous emergency thinks with his legs.

CRAFT, *n.*
A fool's substitute for brains.

CREDITOR, *n.*
One of a tribe of savages dwelling beyond the Financial Straits and dreaded for their desolating incursions.

CUNNING, *n.*
The faculty that distinguishes a weak animal or person from a strong one. It brings its possessor much mental satisfaction and great material adversity. An Italian proverb says: "The furrier gets the skins of more foxes than asses."

CYNIC, *n.*
A blackguard whose faulty vision sees things as they are, not as they ought to be. Hence the custom among the Scythians of plucking out a cynic's eyes to improve his vision.

COWARD

D

DAMN, *v.*
A word formerly much used by the Paphlagonians, the meaning of which is lost. By the learned Dr. Dolabelly Gak it is believed to have been a term of satisfaction, implying the highest possible degree of mental tranquillity. Professor Groke, on the contrary, thinks it expressed an emotion of tumultuous delight, because it so frequently occurs in combination with the word *jod* or *god*, meaning "joy." It would be with great diffidence that I should advance an opinion conflicting with that of either of these formidable authorities.

DANCE, *v. i.*
To leap about to the sound of tittering music, preferably with arms about your neighbor's wife or daughter. There are many kinds of dances, but all those requiring the participation of the two sexes have two characteristics in common: they are conspicuously innocent, and warmly loved by the vicious.

DARING, *n.*
One of the most conspicuous qualities of a man in security.

DATARY, *n.*
A high ecclesiastic official of the Roman Catholic Church, whose important function is to brand the Pope's bulls with the words *Datum Romae.* He enjoys a princely revenue and the friendship of God.

DAWN, *n.*
The time when men of reason go to bed. Certain old men prefer to rise at about that time, taking a cold bath and a long walk with an empty stomach, and otherwise mortifying the flesh. They then point with pride to these practices as the cause of their sturdy health and ripe years; the truth being that they are hearty and old, not because of their habits, but in spite of them.

DAWN

The reason we find only robust persons doing this thing is that it has killed all the others who have tried it.

DAY, *n.*
A period of twenty-four hours, mostly misspent. This period is divided into two parts, the day proper and the night, or day improper—the former devoted to sins of business, the latter consecrated to the other sort. These two kinds of social activity overlap.

DEAD, *adj.*

Done with the work of breathing; done
With all the world; the mad race run
Through to the end; the golden goal
Attained and found to be a hole!
Squatol Johnes.

DEBAUCHEE, *n.*
One who has so earnestly pursued pleasure that he has had the misfortune to overtake it.

DANCE

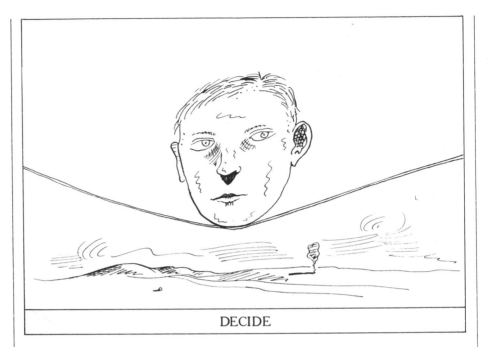

DECIDE

DEBT, *n.*
An ingenious substitute for the chain and whip of the slave-driver.

> As, pent in an aquarium, the troutlet
> Swims round and round his tank to find an outlet,
> Pressing his nose against the glass that holds him,
> Nor ever sees the prison that enfolds him;
> So the poor debtor, seeing naught around him,
> Yet feels the narrow limits that impound him,
> Grieves at his debt and studies to evade it,
> And finds at last he might as well have paid it.
> *Barlow S. Vode.*

DECIDE, *v. i.*
To succumb to the preponderance of one set of influences over another set.

> A leaf was riven from a tree,
> "I mean to fall to earth," said he.
>
> The west wind, rising, made him veer.
> "Eastward," said he, "I now shall steer."

> The east wind rose with greater force.
> Said he: " 'Twere wise to change my course."
>
> With equal power they contend.
> He said: "My judgment I suspend."
>
> Down died the winds; the leaf, elate,
> Cried: "I've decided to fall straight."
>
> "First thoughts are best?" That's not the moral;
> Just choose your own and we'll not quarrel.
>
> Howe'er your choice may chance to fall,
> You'll have no hand in it at all.
> *G. J.*

DEFAME, *v. t.*
To lie about another. To tell the truth about another.

DEFENCELESS, *adj.*
Unable to attack.

DEGENERATE, *adj.*
Less conspicuously admirable than one's ancestors. The contemporaries of Homer were striking examples of degeneracy; it required ten of them to raise a rock or a riot that one of the heroes of the Trojan war could have raised with ease. Homer never tires of sneering at "men who live in these degenerate days," which is perhaps why they suffered him to beg his bread—a marked instance of returning good for evil, by the way, for if they had forbidden him he would certainly have starved.

DEGRADATION, *n.*
One of the stages of moral and social progress from private station to political preferment.

DEINOTHERIUM, *n.*
An extinct pachyderm that flourished when the Pterodactyl was in fashion. The latter was a native of Ireland, its name being pronounced Terry Dactyl or Peter O'Dactyl, as the man pronouncing it may chance to have heard it spoken or seen it printed.

DEJEUNER, *n.*
The breakfast of an American who has been in Paris. Variously pronounced.

DELEGATION, *n.*
In American politics, an article of merchandise that comes in sets.

DELIBERATION, *n.*
The act of examining one's bread to determine which side it is buttered on.

DELUGE, *n.*
A notable first experiment in baptism which washed away the sins (and sinners) of the world.

DELUSION

DELUSION, *n.*
The father of a most respectable family, comprising Enthusiasm, Affection, Self-denial, Faith, Hope, Charity and many other goodly sons and daughters.

> All hail, Delusion! Were it not for
>   thee
> The world turned topsy-turvy we
>   should see;
> For Vice, respectable with cleanly
>   fancies,
> Would fly abandoned Virtue's gross
>   advances.
>   *Mumfrey Mappel.*

DENTIST, *n.*
A prestidigitator who, putting metal into your mouth, pulls coins out of your pocket.

DEPENDENT, *adj.*
Reliant upon another's generosity for the support which you are not in a position to exact from his fears.

DEPUTY, *n.*
A male relative of an officeholder, or of his bondsman. The deputy is commonly a beautiful young man, with a red necktie and an intricate system of cobwebs extending from his nose to his desk. When accidentally struck by the janitor's broom, he gives off a cloud of dust.

DESTINY, *n.*
A tyrant's authority for crime and a
fool's excuse for failure.

DIAGNOSIS, *n.*
A physician's forecast of disease by
the patient's pulse and purse.

DIAPHRAGM, *n.*
A muscular partition separating
disorders of the chest from
disorders of the bowels.

DICTATOR, *n.*
The chief of a nation that prefers
the pestilence of despotism to the
plague of anarchy.

DICTIONARY, *n.*
A malevolent literary device for
cramping the growth of a language
and making it hard and inelastic.
This dictionary, however, is a most
useful work.

DIE, *n.*
The singular of "dice." We seldom
hear the word, because there is a
prohibitory proverb, "Never say
die." At long intervals, however,
some one says: "The die is cast,"
which is not true, for it is cut. The
word is found in an immortal
couplet by that eminent poet and
domestic economist, Senator
Depew:

> A cube of cheese no larger than a
>   die
> May bait the trap to catch a
>   nibbling mie.

DIGESTION, *n.*
The conversion of victuals into
virtues. When the process is
imperfect, vices are evolved
instead—a circumstance from
which that wicked writer, Dr.
Jeremiah Blenn, infers that the
ladies are the greater sufferers
from dyspepsia.

DOG, *n.*
A kind of additional or subsidiary
Deity designed to catch the
overflow and surplus of the world's
worship. This Divine Being in some
of his smaller and silkier
incarnations takes, in the affection
of Woman, the place to which there
is no human male aspirant. The
Dog is a survival—an anachronism.
He toils not, neither does he spin,
yet Solomon in all his glory never
lay upon a door-mat all day long,
sun-soaked and fly-fed and fat,
while his master worked for the
means wherewith to purchase an
idle wag of the Solomonic tail,
seasoned with a look of tolerant
recognition.

DULLARD, *n.*
A member of the reigning dynasty
in letters and life. The Dullards
came in with Adam, and being both
numerous and sturdy have overrun
the habitable world. The secret of
their power is their insensibility to
blows; tickle them with a bludgeon
and they laugh with a platitude.
The Dullards came originally from
Boeotia, whence they were driven
by stress of starvation, their dulness
having blighted the crops. For some
centuries they infested Philistia,
and many of them are called
Philistines to this day. In the
turbulent times of the Crusades
they withdrew thence and
gradually overspread all Europe,
occupying most of the high places
in politics, art, literature, science
and theology. Since a detachment of
Dullards came over with the
Pilgrims in the *Mayflower* and
made a favorable report of the
country, their increase by birth,
immigration, and conversion has
been rapid and steady. According
to the most trustworthy statistics
the number of adult Dullards in the
United States is but little short of
thirty millions, including the
statisticians. The intellectual centre
of the race is somewhere about
Peoria, Illinois.

DESTINY

E

EAT, *v. i.*
To perform successively (and successfully) the functions of mastication, humectation, and deglutition.

"I was in the drawing-room, enjoying my dinner," said Brillat-Savarin, beginning an anecdote. "What!" interrupted Rochebriant; "eating dinner in a drawing-room?" "I must beg you to observe, monsieur," explained the great gastronome, "that I did not say I was eating my dinner, but enjoying it. I had dined an hour before."

EAVESDROP, *v. i.*
Secretly to overhear a catalogue of the crimes and vices of another or yourself.

ECCENTRICITY, *n.*
A method of distinction so cheap that fools employ it to accentuate their incapacity.

ECCENTRICITY

ECONOMY, *n.*
Purchasing the barrel of whiskey that you do not need for the price of the cow that you cannot afford.

EDIBLE, *adj.*
Good to eat, and wholesome to digest, as a worm to a toad, a toad to a snake, a snake to a pig, a pig to a man, and a man to a worm.

EDITOR, *n.*
A person who combines the judicial functions of Minos, Rhadamanthus and Aeacus, but is placable with an obolus; a severely virtuous censor, but so charitable withal that he tolerates the virtues of others and the vices of himself; who flings about him the splintering lightning and sturdy thunders of admonition till he resembles a bunch of firecrackers petulantly uttering its mind at the tail of a dog; then straightway murmurs a mild, melodious lay, soft as the cooing of a donkey intoning its prayer to the evening star. Master of mysteries and lord of law, high-pinnacled upon the throne of thought, his face suffused with the dim splendors of the Transfiguration, his legs intertwisted and his tongue a-cheek, the editor spills his will along the paper and cuts if off in lengths to suit. And at intervals from behind the veil of the temple is heard the voice of the foreman demanding three inches of wit and six lines of religious meditation, or bidding him turn off the wisdom and whack up some pathos.

EDUCATION, *n.*
That which discloses to the wise and disguises from the foolish their lack of understanding.

EFFECT, *n.*
The second of two phenomena which always occur together in the same order. The first, called a Cause, is said to generate the other—which is no more sensible

EDUCATION

than it would be for one who has never seen a dog except in pursuit of a rabbit to declare the rabbit the cause of the dog.

EGOTIST, *n.*
A person of low taste, more interested in himself than in me.

EJECTION, *n.*
An approved remedy for the disease of garrulity. It is also much used in cases of extreme poverty.

ELECTOR, *n.*
One who enjoys the sacred privilege of voting for the man of another man's choice.

ELECTRICITY, *n.*
The power that causes all natural phenomena not known to be caused by something else. It is the same thing as lightning, and its famous attempt to strike Dr. Franklin is one of the most picturesque incidents in that great and good man's career. The memory of Dr. Franklin is justly held in great reverence, particularly in France, where a waxen effigy of him was recently on exhibition, bearing the following touching account of his life and services to science:

"Monsieur Franqulin, inventor of electricity. This illustrious savant, after having made several voyages around the world, died on the Sandwich Islands and was devoured by savages, of whom not a single fragment was ever recovered."

Electricity seems destined to play a most important part in the arts and industries. The question of its economical application to some purposes is still unsettled, but experiment has already proved that it will propel a street car better than a gas jet and give more light than a horse.

ELEGY, *n.*
A composition in verse, in which, without employing any of the methods of humor, the writer aims to produce in the reader's mind the dampest kind of dejection. The most famous English example begins somewhat like this:

> The cur foretells the knell of parting day;
> The loafing herd winds slowly o'er the lea;
> The wise man homeward plods; I only stay
> To fiddle-faddle in a minor key.

ELOQUENCE, *n.*
The art of orally persuading fools that white is the color that it appears to be. It includes the gift of making any color appear white.

ELYSIUM, *n.*
An imaginary delightful country which the ancients foolishly believed to be inhabited by the spirits of the good. This ridiculous and mischievous fable was swept off the face of the earth by the early Christians—may their souls be happy in Heaven!

EMANCIPATION, *n.*
A bondsman's change from the tyranny of another to the despotism of himself.

EMBALM, *v. t.*
To cheat vegetation by locking up
the gases upon which it feeds. By
embalming their dead and thereby
deranging the natural balance
between animal and vegetable life,
the Egyptians made their once
fertile and populous country barren
and incapable of supporting more
than a meagre crew. The modern
metallic burial casket is a step in
the same direction, and many a
dead man who ought now to be
ornamenting his neighbor's lawn as
a tree, or enriching his table as a
bunch of radishes, is doomed to a
long inutility. We shall get him
after awhile if we are spared, but
in the meantime the violet and rose
are languishing for a nibble at his
glutoeus maximus.

EMOTION, *n.*
A prostrating disease caused by a
determination of the heart to the
head. It is sometimes accompanied
by a copious discharge of hydrated
chloride of sodium from the eyes.

ENCOMIAST, *n.*
A special (but not particular) kind
of liar.

END, *n.*
The position farthest removed on
either hand from the Interlocutor.

> The man was perishing apace
> Who played the tambourine:
> The seal of death was on his face—
> 'Twas pallid, for 'twas clean.
>
> "This is the end," the sick man said
> In faint and failing tones.
> A moment later he was dead,
> And Tambourine was Bones.
> *Tinley Roquot.*

ENOUGH, *pro.*
All there is in the world if you like it.

> Enough is as good as a feast—for
> that matter
> Enougher's as good as a feast and
> the platter.
> *Arbely C. Strunk.*

ENTERTAINMENT, *n.*
Any kind of amusement whose
inroads stop short of death by
dejection.

ENTHUSIASM, *n.*
A distemper of youth, curable by
small doses of repentance in
connection with outward
applications of experience. Byron,
who recovered long enough to call it
"entuzy-muzy," had a relapse which
carried him off—to Missolonghi.

ENVELOPE, *n.*
The coffin of a document; the
scabbard of a bill; the husk of a
remittance; the bed-gown of a love-
letter.

ENVY, *n.*
Emulation adapted to the meanest
capacity.

EPAULET, *n.*
An ornamented badge, serving to
distinguish a military officer from
the enemy—that is to say, from the
officer of lower rank to whom his
death would give promotion.

EPICURE, *n.*
An opponent of Epicurus, an
abstemious philosopher who,
holding that pleasure should be the
chief aim of man, wasted no time in
gratification of the senses.

ESOTERIC, *adj.*
Very particularly abstruse and
consummately occult. The ancient
philosophies were of two kinds,—
exoteric, those that the philosophers
themselves could partly understand,
and *esoteric*, those that nobody
could understand. It is the latter
that have most profoundly affected
modern thought and found greatest
acceptance in our time.

ESOTERIC

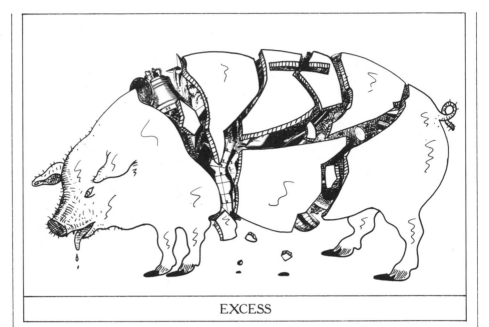

EXCESS

ETHNOLOGY, *n.*
The science that treats of the various tribes of Man, as robbers, thieves, swindlers, dunces, lunatics, idiots and ethnologists.

EUCHARIST, *n.*
A sacred feast of the religious sect of Theophagi.

A dispute once unhappily arose among the members of this sect as to what it was that they ate. In this controversy some five hundred thousand have already been slain, and the question is still unsettled.

EULOGY, *n.*
Praise of a person who has either the advantages of wealth and power, or the consideration to be dead.

EXCEPTION, *n.*
A thing which takes the liberty to differ from other things of its class, as an honest man, a truthful woman, etc. "The exception proves the rule" is an expression constantly upon the lips of the ignorant, who parrot it from one another with never a thought of its absurdity. In the Latin, *"Exceptio probat regulam"* means that the exception *tests* the rule, puts it to the proof, not *confirms* it. The malefactor who drew the meaning from this excellent dictum and substituted a contrary one of his own exerted an evil power which appears to be immortal.

EXCESS, *n.*
In morals, an indulgence that enforces by appropriate penalties the law of moderation.

EXCOMMUNICATION, *n.*

This "excommunication" is a word
In speech ecclesiastical oft heard,
And means the damning, with bell,
    book and candle,
Some sinner whose opinions are a
    scandal—
A rite permitting Satan to enslave him
Forever, and forbidding Christ to save
    him.
                              Gat Huckle.

EXECUTIVE, *n.*
An officer of the Government, whose duty it is to enforce the wishes of the legislative power until such time as the judicial department shall be pleased to pronounce them invalid and of no effect. Following is an extract from an old book entitled, *The Lunarian Astonished* — Pfeiffer & Co., Boston, 1803:

LUNARIAN: Then when your Congress has passed a law it goes directly to the Supreme Court in order that it may at once be known whether it is constitutional?

TERRESTRIAN: O no; it does not require the approval of the Supreme Court until having perhaps been enforced for many years somebody objects to its operation against himself — I mean his client. The President, if he approves it, begins to execute it at once.

LUNARIAN: Ah, the executive power is a part of the legislative. Do your policemen also have to approve the local ordinances that they enforce?

TERRESTRIAN: Not yet — at least not in their character of constables. Generally speaking, though, all laws require the approval of those whom they are intended to restrain.

LUNARIAN: I see. The death warrant is not valid until signed by the murderer.

TERRESTRIAN: My friend, you put it too strongly; we are not so consistent.

LUNARIAN: But this system of maintaining an expensive judicial machinery to pass upon the validity of laws only after they have long been executed, and then only when brought before the court by some private person — does it not cause great confusion?

TERRESTRIAN: It does.

LUNARIAN: Why then should not your laws, previously to being executed, be validated, not by the signature of your President, but by that of the Chief Justice of the Supreme Court?

TERRESTRIAN: There is no precedent for any such course.

LUNARIAN: Precedent. What is that?

TERRESTRIAN: It has been defined by five hundred lawyers in three volumes each. So how can any one know?

EXHORT, *v. t.*
In religious affairs, to put the conscience of another upon the spit and roast it to a nut-brown discomfort.

EXILE, *n.*
One who serves his country by residing abroad, yet is not an ambassador.

An English sea-captain being asked if he had read "The Exile of Erin," replied: "No, sir, but I should like to anchor on it." Years afterwards, when he had been hanged as a pirate after a career of unparalleled atrocities, the following memorandum was found in the ship's log that he had kept at the time of his reply:

Aug. 3d, 1842. Made a joke on the ex-Isle of Erin. Coldly received. War with the whole world!

EXISTENCE, *n.*

A transient, horrible, fantastic
  dream,
Wherein is nothing yet all things do
  seem:
From which we're wakened by a
  friendly nudge
Of our bedfellow Death, and cry: "O
  fudge!"

EXPERIENCE, *n.*
The wisdom that enables us to recognize as an undesirable old acquaintance the folly that we have already embraced.

To one who, journeying through
  night and fog,
Is mired neck-deep in an
  unwholesome bog,
Experience, like the rising of the
  dawn,
Reveals the path that he should not
  have gone.
                    Joel Frad Bink.

EXPOSTULATION, *n.*
One of the many methods by which fools prefer to lose their friends.

EXTINCTION, *n.*
The raw material out of which theology created the future state.

F

FAIRY, *n.*
A creature, variously fashioned and endowed, that formerly inhabited the meadows and forests. It was nocturnal in its habits, and somewhat addicted to dancing and the theft of children. The fairies are now believed by naturalists to be extinct, though a clergyman of the Church of England saw three near Colchester as lately as 1855, while passing through a park after dining with the lord of the manor. The sight greatly staggered him, and he was so affected that his account of it was incoherent. In the year 1807 a troop of fairies visited a wood near Aix and carried off the daughter of a peasant, who had been seen to enter it with a bundle of clothing. The son of a wealthy *bourgeois* disappeared about the same time, but afterward returned. He had seen the abduction and been in pursuit of the fairies. Justinian Gaux, a writer of the fourteenth century, avers that so great is the fairies' power of transformation that he saw one change itself into two opposing armies and fight a battle with great slaughter, and that the next day, after it had resumed its original shape and gone away, there were seven hundred bodies of the slain which the villagers had to bury. He does not say if any of the wounded recovered. In the time of Henry III, of England, a law was made which prescribed the death penalty for "Kyllynge,wowndynge, or mamynge" a fairy, and it was universally respected.

FAITH, *n.*
Belief without evidence in what is told by one who speaks without knowledge, of things without parallel.

FAMOUS, *adj.*
Conspicuously miserable.

FASHION, *n.*
A despot whom the wise ridicule and obey.

FEAST, *n.*
A festival. A religious celebration usually signalized by gluttony and drunkenness, frequently in honor of some holy person distinguished for abstemiousness. In the Roman Catholic Church feasts are "movable" and "immovable," but the celebrants are uniformly immovable until they are full. In their earliest development these entertainments took the form of feasts for the dead; such were held by the Greeks, under the name of *Nemeseia*, by the Aztecs and Peruvians, as in modern times they are popular with the Chinese; though it is believed that the ancient dead, like the modern, were light eaters. Among the many feasts of the Romans was the *Novemdiale*, which was held, according to Livy, whenever stones fell from heaven.

FELON, *n.*
A person of greater enterprise than discretion, who in embracing an opportunity has formed an unfortunate attachment.

FICKLENESS, *n.*
The iterated satiety of an enterprising affection.

FIDDLE, *n.*
An instrument to tickle human ears by friction of a horse's tail on the entrails of a cat.

FIDELITY, *n.*
A virtue peculiar to those who are about to be betrayed.

FAMOUS

FINANCE, *n.*
The art or science of managing revenues and resources for the best advantage of the manager. The pronunciation of this word with the i long and the accent on the first syllable is one of America's most precious discoveries and possessions.

FLAG, *n.*
A colored rag borne above troops and hoisted on forts and ships. It appears to serve the same purpose as certain signs that one sees on vacant lots in London—"Rubbish may be shot here."

FLESH, *n.*
The Second Person of the secular Trinity.

FLY-SPECK, *n.*
The prototype of punctuation. It is observed by Garvinus that the systems of punctuation in use by the various literary nations depended originally upon the social habits and general diet of the flies infesting the several countries. These creatures, which have always been distinguished for a neighborly and companionable familiarity with authors, liberally or niggardly embellish the manuscripts in process of growth under the pen, according to their bodily habit, bringing out the sense of the work by a species of interpretation superior to, and independent of, the writer's powers. The "old masters" of literature—that is to say, the early writers whose work is so esteemed by later scribes and critics in the same language— never punctuated at all, but worked right along free-handed, without that abruption of the thought which comes from the use of points. (We observe the same thing in children

to-day, whose usage in this particular is a striking and beautiful instance of the law that the infancy of individuals reproduces the methods and stages of development characterizing the infancy of races.) In the work of these primitive scribes all the punctuation is found, by the modern investigator with his optical instruments and chemical tests, to have been inserted by the writers' ingenious and serviceable collaborator, the common house-fly—*Musca maledicta.* In transcribing these ancient MSS, for the purpose of either making the work their own or preserving what they naturally regard as divine revelations, later writers reverently and accurately copy whatever marks they find upon the papyrus or parchment, to the unspeakable enhancement of the lucidity of the thought and value of the work. Writers contemporary with the copyists naturally avail themselves of the obvious advantages of these marks in their own work, and with such assistance as the flies of their own household may be willing to grant, frequently rival and sometimes surpass the older compositions, in respect at least of punctuation, which is no small glory. Fully to understand the important services that flies perform to literature it is only necessary to lay a page of some popular novelist alongside a saucer of cream-and-molasses in a sunny room and observe "how the wit brightens and the style refines" in accurate proportion to the duration of exposure.

FOLLY, *n.*
That "gift and faculty divine" whose creative and controlling energy inspires Man's mind, guides his actions and adorns his life.

FOOL, *n.*
A person who pervades the domain of intellectual speculation and

FOOL

diffuses himself through the channels of moral activity. He is omnific, omniform, omnipercipient, omniscient, omnipotent. He it was who invented letters, printing, the railroad, the steamboat, the telegraph, the platitude and the circle of the sciences. He created patriotism and taught the nations war—founded theology, philosophy, law, medicine and Chicago. He established monarchical and republican government. He is from everlasting to everlasting—such as creation's dawn beheld he fooleth now. In the morning of time he sang upon primitive hills, and in the noonday of existence headed the procession of being. His grandmotherly hand has warmly tucked-in the set sun of civilization, and in the twilight he prepares Man's evening meal of milk-and-morality and turns down the covers of the universal grave. And after the rest of us shall have retired for the night of eternal oblivion he will sit up to write a history of human civilization.

FOREFINGER, *n.*
The finger commonly used in pointing out two malefactors.

FOREORDINATION, *n.*
This looks like an easy word to define, but when I consider that pious and learned theologians have spent long lives in explaining it, and written libraries to explain their explanations; when I remember that nations have been divided and bloody battles caused by the difference between foreordination and predestination, and that millions of treasure have been expended in the effort to prove and disprove its compatibility with freedom of the will and the efficacy of prayer, praise, and a religious life, — recalling these awful facts in the history of the word, I stand appalled before the mighty problem of its signification, abase my spiritual eyes, fearing to contemplate its portentous magnitude, reverently uncover and humbly refer it to His Eminence Cardinal Gibbons and His Grace Bishop Potter.

FORGETFULNESS, *n.*
A gift of God bestowed upon debtors in compensation for their destitution of conscience.

FORK, *n.*
An instrument used chiefly for the purpose of putting dead animals into the mouth. Formerly the knife was employed for this purpose, and by many worthy persons is still thought to have many advantages over the other tool, which, however, they do not altogether reject, but use to assist in charging the knife. The immunity of these persons from swift and awful death is one of the most striking proofs of God's mercy to those that hate Him.

FREEDOM, *n.*
Exemption from the stress of authority in a beggarly half dozen of restraint's infinite multitude of methods. A political condition that every nation supposes itself to enjoy in virtual monopoly. Liberty. The distinction between freedom and liberty is not accurately known; naturalists have never been able to find a living specimen of either.

> Freedom, as every schoolboy knows,
>   Once shrieked as Kosciusko fell;
> On every wind, indeed, that blows
>   I hear her yell.
>
> She screams whenever monarchs meet,
>   And parliaments as well,
> To bind the chains about her feet
>   And toll her knell.
>
> And when the sovereign people cast
>   The votes they cannot spell,
> Upon the pestilential blast
>   Her clamors swell.
>
> For all to whom the power's given
>   To sway or to compel,
> Among themselves apportion Heaven
>   And give her Hell.
>   *Blary O'Gary.*

FREEMASONS, *n.*
An order with secret rites, grotesque ceremonies and fantastic costumes, which, originating in the reign of Charles II, among working artisans of London, has been joined successively by the dead of past centuries in unbroken retrogression until now it embraces all the generations of man on the hither side of Adam and is drumming up distinguished recruits among the pre-Creational inhabitants of Chaos and the Formless Void. The order was founded at different times by Charlemagne, Julius Caesar, Cyrus, Solomon, Zoroaster, Confucius, Thothmes, and Buddha. Its emblems and symbols have been found in the Catacombs of Paris and Rome, on the stones of the Parthenon and the Chinese Great Wall, among the temples of Karnak and Palmyra and in the Egyptian Pyramids—always by a Freemason.

FRIENDLESS, *adj.*
Having no favors to bestow.
Destitute of fortune. Addicted to
utterance of truth and common
sense.

FRIENDSHIP, *n.*
A ship big enough to carry two in
fair weather, but only one in foul.

FROG, *n.*
A reptile with edible legs. The first
mention of frogs in profane
literature is in Homer's narrative of
the war between them and the
mice. Skeptical persons have
doubted Homer's authorship of the
work, but the learned, ingenious
and industrious Dr. Schliemann has
set the question forever at rest by
uncovering the bones of the slain
frogs. One of the forms of moral
suasion by which Pharaoh was
besought to favor the Israelities was
a plague of frogs, but Pharaoh, who
liked them *fricasées*, remarked,
with truly oriental stoicism, that he
could stand it as long as the frogs
and the Jews could; so the
programme was changed. The frog
is a diligent songster, having a good
voice but no ear. The libretto of his
favorite opera, as written by
Aristophanes, is brief, simple and
effective—"brekekex-koäx"; the
music is apparently by that
eminent composer, Richard
Wagner. Horses have a frog in each
hoof—a thoughtful provision of
nature, enabling them to shine in a
hurdle race.

FRYING-PAN, *n.*
One part of the penal apparatus
employed in that punitive
institution, a woman's kitchen. The
frying-pan was invented by Calvin,
and by him used in cooking span-
long infants that had died without
baptism; and observing one day the
horrible torment of a tramp who
had incautiously pulled a fried babe
from the waste-dump and devoured
it, it occurred to the great divine to
rob death of its terrors by
introducing the frying-pan into
every household in Geneva. Thence
it spread to all corners of the world,
and has been of invaluable
assistance in the propagation of his
sombre faith. The following lines
(said to be from the pen of his
Grace Bishop Potter) seem to imply
that the usefulness of this utensil is
not limited to this world; but as the
consequences of its employment in
this life reach over into the life to
come, so also itself may be found on
the other side, rewarding its
devotees:

> Old Nick was summoned to the
> skies.
>   Said Peter: "Your intentions
> Are good, but you lack enterprise
>   Concerning new inventions.
>
> "Now, broiling is an ancient plan
>   Of torment, but I hear it
> Reported that the frying-pan
>   Sears best the wicked spirit.
>
> "Go get one—fill it up with fat—
>   Fry sinners brown and good in't."
> "I know a trick worth two o' that,"
>   Said Nick—"I'll cook their food
>   in't."

FUNERAL, *n.*
A pageant whereby we attest our
respect for the dead by enriching
the undertaker, and strengthen our
grief by an expenditure that
deepens our groans and doubles our
tears.

> The savage dies—they sacrifice a
>   horse
> To bear to happy hunting-grounds
>   the corse.
> Our friends expire—we make the
>   money fly
> In hope their souls will chase it to
>   the sky.
>   *Jex Wopley.*

FUTURE, *n.*
That period of time in which our
affairs prosper, our friends are true
and our happiness is assured.

G

GALLOWS, *n.*
A stage for the performance of miracle plays, in which the leading actor is translated to heaven. In this country the gallows is chiefly remarkable for the number of persons who escape it.

> Whether on the gallows high
>   Or where blood flows the reddest,
> The noblest place for man to die —
>   Is where he died the deadest.
> *Old Play.*

GARGOYLE, *n.*
A rain-spout projecting from the eaves of mediaeval buildings, commonly fashioned into a grotesque caricature of some personal enemy of the architect or owner of the building. This was especially the case in churches and ecclesiastical structures generally, in which the gargoyles presented a perfect rogues' gallery of local heretics and controversialists. Sometimes when a new dean and chapter were installed the old gargoyles were removed and others substituted having a closer relation to the private animosities of the new incumbents.

GARTER, *n.*
An elastic band intended to keep a woman from coming out of her stockings and desolating the country.

GENEALOGY, *n.*
An account of one's descent from an ancestor who did not particularly care to trace his own.

GENEROUS, *adj.*
Originally this word meant noble by birth and was rightly applied to a great multitude of persons. It now means noble by nature and is taking a bit of a rest.

GENTEEL, *adj.*
Refined, after the fashion of a gent.

GENTEEL

GEOGRAPHER, *n.*
A chap who can tell you offhand the difference between the outside of the world and the inside.

GEOLOGY, *n.*
The science of the earth's crust — to which, doubtless, will be added that of its interior whenever a man shall come up garrulous out of a well. The geological formations of the globe already noted are catalogued thus: The Primary, or lower one, consists of rocks, bones of mired mules, gas-pipes, miners' tools, antique statues minus the nose, Spanish doubloons and ancestors. The Secondary is largely made up of red worms and moles. The Tertiary comprises railway tracks, patent pavements, grass, snakes, mouldy boots, beer bottles, tomato cans, intoxicated citizens, garbage, anarchists, snap-dogs and fools.

GHOST, *n.*
The outward and visible sign of an inward fear.

GLUTTON, *n.*
A person who escapes the evils of moderation by committing dyspepsia.

GNOSTICS, *n.*
A sect of philosophers who tried to engineer a fusion between the early Christians and the Platonists. The former would not go into the caucus and the combination failed, greatly to the chagrin of the fusion managers.

GNU, *n.*
An animal of South Africa, which in its domesticated state resembles a horse, a buffalo and a stag. In its wild condition it is something like a thunderbolt, an earthquake and a cyclone.

GOOD, *adj.*
Sensible, madam, to the worth of this present writer. Alive, sir, to the advantages of letting him alone.

GOOSE, *n.*
A bird that supplies quills for writing. These, by some occult process of nature, are penetrated and suffused with various degrees of the bird's intellectual energies and emotional character, so that when inked and drawn mechanically across paper by a person called an "author," there results a very fair and accurate transcript of the fowl's thought and feeling. The difference in geese, as discovered by this ingenious method, is considerable: many are found to have only trivial and insignificant powers, but some are seen to be very great geese indeed.

GOUT, *n.*
A physician's name for the rheumatism of a rich patient.

GRAMMAR, *n.*
A system of pitfalls thoughtfully prepared for the feet of the self-made man, along the path by which he advances to distinction.

GRAVITATION, *n.*
The tendency of all bodies to approach one another with a strength proportioned to the quantity of matter they contain—the quantity of matter they contain being ascertained by the strength of their tendency to approach one another. This is a lovely and edifying illustration of how science, having made A the proof of B, makes B the proof of A.

GUILLOTINE, *n.*
A machine which makes a Frenchman shrug his shoulders with good reason.

In his great work on *Divergent Lines of Racial Evolution*, the learned Professor Brayfugle argues from the prevalence of this gesture—the shrug—among Frenchmen, that they are descended from turtles and it is simply a survival of the habit of retracting the head inside the shell. It is with reluctance that I differ with so eminent an authority, but in my judgment (as more elaborately set forth and enforced in my work entitled *Hereditary Emotions*—lib. II, c. XI) the shrug is a poor foundation upon which to build so important a theory, for previously to the Revolution the gesture was unknown. I have not a doubt that it is directly referable to the terror inspired by the guillotine during the period of that instrument's activity.

GRAVITATION

HABEAS CORPUS
A writ by which a man may be taken out of jail when confined for the wrong crime.

HABIT, n.
A shackle for the free.

HALF, n.
One of two equal parts into which a thing may be divided, or considered as divided. In the fourteenth century a heated discussion arose among theologians and philosophers as to whether Omniscience could part an object into three halves; and the pious Father Aldrovinus publicly prayed in the cathedral at Rouen that God would demonstrate the affirmative of the proposition in some signal and unmistakable way, and particularly (if it should please Him) upon the body of that hardy blasphemer, Manutius Procinus, who maintained the negative. Procinus, however, was spared to die of the bite of a viper.

HALO, n.
Properly, a luminous ring encircling an astronomical body, but not infrequently confounded with "aureola," or "nimbus," a somewhat similar phenomenon worn as a head-dress by divinities and saints. The halo is a purely optical illusion, produced by moisture in the air, in the manner of a rainbow; but the aureola is conferred as a sign of superior sanctity, in the same way as a bishop's mitre, or the Pope's tiara.

HAND, n.
A singular instrument worn at the end of the human arm and commonly thrust into somebody's pocket.

HANDKERCHIEF, n.
A small square of silk or linen, used in various ignoble offices about the face and especially serviceable at funerals to conceal the lack of tears. The handkerchief is of recent invention; our ancestors knew nothing of it and intrusted its duties to the sleeve. Shakespeare's introducing it into the play of "Othello" is an anachronism: Desdemona dried her nose with her skirt, as Dr. Mary Walker and other reformers have done with their coattails in our own day—an evidence that revolutions sometimes go backward.

HANGMAN, n.
An officer of the law charged with duties of the highest dignity and utmost gravity, and held in hereditary disesteem by a populace having a criminal ancestry. In some of the American States his functions are now performed by an electrician, as in New Jersey, where executions by electricity have recently been ordered—the first instance known to this lexicographer of anybody questioning the expediency of hanging Jerseymen.

HAPPINESS, n.
An agreeable sensation arising from contemplating the misery of another.

HARANGUE, n.
A speech by an opponent, who is known as an harangue-outang.

HARBOR, n.
A place where ships taking shelter from storms are exposed to the fury of the customs.

HARMONISTS, n.
A sect of Protestants, now extinct, who came from Europe in the beginning of the last century and were distinguished for the bitterness of their internal controversies and dissensions.

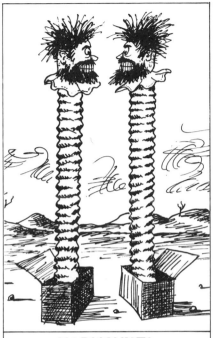

HARMONISTS

which a beefsteak becomes a feeling—tender or not, according to the age of the animal from which it was cut; the successive stages of elaboration through which a caviar sandwich is transmuted to a quaint fancy and reappears as a pungent epigram; the marvelous functional methods of converting a hard-boiled egg into religious contrition, or a cream-puff into a sigh of sensibility—these things have been patiently ascertained by M. Pasteur, and by him expounded with convincing lucidity. (See, also, my monograph, *The Essential Identity of the Spiritual Affections and Certain Intestinal Gases Freed in Digestion*—4to, 687 pp.) In a scientific work entitled, I believe, *Delectatio Demonorum* (John Camden Hotton, London, 1873) this view of the sentiments receives a striking illustration; and for further light consult Professor Dam's famous treatise on *Love as a Product of Alimentary Maceration.*

HASH, *x.*
There is no definition for this word—nobody knows what hash is.

HATRED, *n.*
A sentiment appropriate to the occasion of another's superiority.

HEAD-MONEY, *n.*
A capitation tax, or poll-tax.

HEARSE, *n.*
Death's baby-carriage.

HEART, *n.*
An automatic, muscular blood pump. Figuratively, this useful organ is said to be the seat of emotions and sentiments—a very pretty fancy which, however, is nothing but a survival of a once universal belief. It is now known that the sentiments and emotions reside in the stomach, being evolved from food by chemical action of the gastric fluid.The exact process by

HEATHEN, *n.*
A benighted creature who has the folly to worship something that he can see and feel. According to Professor Howison, of the California State University, Hebrews are heathens.

HEAVEN, *n.*
A place where the wicked cease from troubling you with talk of their personal affairs, and the good listen with attention while you expound your own.

HEBREW, *n.*
A male Jew, as distinguished from the Shebrew, an altogether superior creation.

HEMP, *n.*
A plant from whose fibrous bark is made an article of neckwear which is frequently put on after public speaking in the open air and prevents the wearer from taking cold.

HERMIT

HERMIT, *n.*
A person whose vices and follies are not sociable.

HERS, *pron.*
His.

HIBERNATE, *v. i.*
To pass the winter season in domestic seclusion. There have been many singular popular notions about the hibernation of various animals. Many believe that the bear hibernates during the whole winter and subsists by mechanically sucking its paws. It is admitted that it comes out of its retirement in the spring so lean that it has to try twice before it can cast a shadow. Three or four centuries ago, in England, no fact was better attested than that swallows passed the winter months in the mud at the bottoms of the brooks, clinging together in globular masses. They have apparently been compelled to give up the custom on account of the foulness of the brooks. Sotus Escobius discovered in Central Asia a whole nation of people who hibernate. By some investigators, the fasting of Lent is supposed to have been originally a modified form of hibernation, to which the Church gave a religious significance; but this view was strenuously opposed by that eminent authority, Bishop Kip, who did not wish any honors denied to the memory of the Founder of his family.

HIPPOGRIFF, *n.*
An animal (now extinct) which was half horse and half griffin. The griffin was itself a compound creature, half lion and half eagle. The hippogriff was actually, therefore, only one-quarter eagle, which is two dollars and fifty cents in gold. The study of zoology is full of surprises.

HISTORIAN, *n.*
A broad-gauge gossip.

HISTORY, *n.*
An account mostly false, of events mostly unimportant, which are brought about by rulers mostly knaves, and soldiers mostly fools.

> Of Roman history, great Niebuhr's shown
> 'Tis nine-tenths lying. Faith, I wish 'twere known,
> Ere we accept great Niebuhr as a guide,
> Wherein he blundered and how much he lied.
>
> *Salder Bupp.*

HOG, *n.*
A bird remarkable for the catholicity of its appetite and serving to illustrate that of ours. Among the Mahometans and Jews, the hog is not in favor as an article of diet, but is respected for the delicacy of its habits, the beauty of its plumage and the melody of its voice. It is chiefly as a songster that the fowl is esteemed; a cage of him in full chorus has been known to draw tears from two persons at once. The scientific name of this dicky-bird is *Porcus Rockefelleri.* Mr. Rockefeller did not discover the hog, but it is considered his by right of resemblance.

HOMICIDE, *n.*
The slaying of one human being by another. There are four kinds of homicide: felonious, excusable, justifiable and praiseworthy, but it

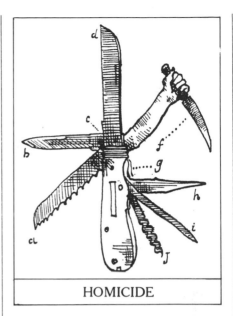

HOMICIDE

makes no great difference to the person slain whether he fell by one kind or another—the classification is for advantage of the lawyers.

HOMOEOPATHY, *n.*
A school of medicine midway between Allopathy and Christian Science. To the last both the others are distinctly inferior, for Christian Science will cure imaginary diseases, and they can not.

HOMOEOPATHIST, *n.*
The humorist of the medical profession.

HONORABLE, *adj.*
Afflicted with an impediment in one's reach. In legislative bodies it is customary to mention all members as honorable; as, "the honorable gentleman is a scurvy cur."

HOPE, *n.*
Desire and expectation rolled into one.

HOSPITALITY, *n.*
The virtue which induces us to feed and lodge certain persons who are not in need of food and lodging.

HOSTILITY, *n.*
A peculiarly sharp and specially applied sense of the earth's overpopulation. Hostility is classed as active and passive; as (respectively) the feeling of a woman for her female friends, and that which she entertains for all the rest of her sex.

HOURI, *n.*
A comely female inhabiting the Mohammedan Paradise to make things cheery for the good Mussulman, whose belief in her existence marks a noble discontent with his earthly spouse, whom he denies a soul. By that good lady the Houris are said to be held in deficient esteem.

HOUSE, *n.*
A hollow edifice erected for the habitation of man, rat, mouse, beetle, cockroach, fly, mosquito, flea, bacillus and microbe. *House of Correction,* a place of reward for political and personal service, and for the detention of offenders and appropriations. *House of God,* a building with a steeple and a mortgage on it. *House-dog,* a pestilent beast kept on domestic premises to insult persons passing by and appal the hardy visitor. *House-maid,* a youngerly person of the opposing sex employed to be variously disagreeable and ingeniously unclean in the station in which it has pleased God to place her.

HUMANITY, *n.*
The human race, collectively, exclusive of the anthropoid poets.

HUMORIST, *n.*
A plague that would have softened down the hoar austerity of Pharaoh's heart and persuaded him to dismiss Israel with his best wishes, cat-quick.

HURRICANE, *n.*
An atmospheric demonstration once very common but now generally abandoned for the tornado and cyclone. The hurricane is still in popular use in the West Indies and is preferred by certain old-fashioned sea-captains. It is also used in the construction of the upper decks of steamboats, but generally speaking, the hurricane's usefulness has outlasted it.

HURRY, *n.*
The dispatch of bunglers.

HUSBAND, *n.*
One who, having dined, is charged with the care of the plate.

HYBRID, *n.*
A pooled issue.

HYPOCRITE

HYPOCRITE, *n.*
One who, professing virtues that he does not respect, secures the advantage of seeming to be what he despises.

HOUSE

I

I
is the first letter of the alphabet, the first word of the language, the first thought of the mind, the first object of affection. In grammar it is a pronoun of the first person and singular number. Its plural is said to be *We*, but how there can be more than one myself is doubtless clearer to the grammarians than it is to the author of this incomparable dictionary. Conception of two myselves is difficult, but fine. The frank yet graceful use of "I" distinguishes a good writer from a bad; the latter carries it with the manner of a thief trying to cloak his loot.

ICHOR, *n.*
A fluid that serves the gods and goddesses in place of blood.

> Fair Venus, speared by Diomed,
> Restrained the raging chief and
>   said:
> "Behold, rash mortal, whom you've
>   bled —
> Your soul's stained white with
>   ichorshed!"
>
> *Mary Doke.*

ICONOCLAST, *n.*
A breaker of idols, the worshipers whereof are imperfectly gratified by the performance, and most strenuously protest that he unbuildeth but doth not reedify, that he pulleth down but pileth not up. For the poor things would have other idols in place of those he thwacketh upon the mazzard and dispelleth. But the iconoclast saith: "Ye shall have none at all, for ye need them not; and if the rebuilder fooleth round hereabout, behold I will depress the head of him and sit thereon till he squawk it."

IDIOT, *n.*
A member of a large and powerful tribe whose influence in human affairs has always been dominant and controlling. The Idiot's activity is not confined to any special field of thought or action, but "pervades and regulates the whole." He has the last word in everything; his decision is unappealable. He sets the fashions of opinion and taste, dictates the limitations of speech and circumscribes conduct with a dead-line.

IDLENESS, *n.*
A model farm where the devil experiments with seeds of new sins and promotes the growth of staple vices.

IGNORAMUS, *n.*
A person unacquainted with certain kinds of knowledge familiar to yourself, and having certain other kinds that you know nothing about.

> Dumble was an ignoramus,
> Mumble was for learning famous.
> Mumble said one day to Dumble:
> "Ignorance should be more humble.
> Not a spark have you of knowledge
> That was got in any college."
> Dumble said to Mumble: "Truly
> You're self-satisfied unduly.
> Of things in college I'm denied
> A knowledge—you of all beside."
>
> *Borelli.*

ILLUMINATI, *n.*
A sect of Spanish heretics of the latter part of the sixteenth century; so called because they were light weights—*cunctationes illuminati.*

ILLUSTRIOUS, *adj.*
Suitably placed for the shafts of malice, envy and detraction.

IMAGINATION, *n.*
A warehouse of facts, with poet and liar in joint ownership.

IMBECILITY, *n.*
A kind of divine inspiration, or sacred fire affecting censorious critics of this dictionary.

IDIOT

IMMIGRANT

IMMIGRANT, *n.*
An unenlightened person who thinks one country better than another.

IMMORAL, *adj.*
Inexpedient. Whatever in the long run and with regard to the greater number of instances men find to be generally inexpedient comes to be considered wrong, wicked, immoral. If man's notions of right and wrong have any other basis than this of expediency; if they originated, or could have originated, in any other way; if actions have in themselves a moral character apart from, and nowise dependent on, their consequences— then all philosophy is a lie and reason a disorder of the mind.

IMMORTALITY, *n.*

A toy which people cry for,
And on their knees apply for,
Dispute, contend and lie for,
    And if allowed
    Would be right proud
Eternally to die for.   G. J.

IMPALE, *v. t.*
In popular usage to pierce with any weapon which remains fixed in the wound. This, however, is inaccurate; to impale is, properly, to put to death by thrusting an upright sharp stake into the body, the victim being left in a sitting posture. This was a common mode of punishment among many of the nations of antiquity, and is still in high favor in China and other parts of Asia. Down to the beginning of the fifteenth century it was widely employed in "churching" heretics and schismatics. Wolecraft calls it the "stoole of repentynge," and among the common people it was jocularly known as "riding the one legged horse." Ludwig Salzmann informs us that in Tibet impalement is considered the most appropriate punishment for crimes against religion; and although in China it is sometimes awarded for secular offences, it is most frequently adjudged in cases of sacrilege. To the person in actual experience of impalement it must be a matter of minor importance by

what kind of civil or religious dissent he was made acquainted with its discomforts; but doubtless he would feel a certain satisfaction if able to contemplate himself in the character of a weather-cock on the spire of the True Church.

IMPARTIAL, *adj.*
Unable to perceive any promise of personal advantage from espousing either side of a controversy or adopting either of two conflicting opinions.

IMPENITENCE, *n.*
A state of mind intermediate in point of time between sin and punishment.

IMPIETY, *n.*
Your irreverence toward my deity.

IMPOSITION, *n.*
The act of blessing or consecrating by the laying on of hands—a ceremony common to many ecclesiastical systems, but performed with the frankest sincerity by the sect known as Thieves.

   "Lo! by the laying on of hands,"
     Say parson, priest and dervise,
   "We consecrate your cash and lands
     To ecclesiastic service.
   No doubt you'll swear till all is blue
   At such an imposition. Do."
             Pollo Doncas.

IMPOSTOR, *n.*
A rival aspirant to public honors.

IMPROVIDENCE, *n.*
Provision for the needs of to-day from the revenues of to-morrow.

IMPUNITY, *n.*
Wealth.

INADMISSIBLE, *adj.*
Not competent to be considered. Said of certain kinds of testimony which juries are supposed to be unfit to be entrusted with, and which judges, therefore, rule out, even of proceedings before themselves alone. Hearsay evidence is inadmissible because the person quoted was unsworn and is not before the court for examination; yet most momentous actions, military, political, commercial and of every other kind, are daily undertaken on hearsay evidence. There is no religion in the world that has any other basis than hearsay evidence. Revelation is hearsay evidence; that the Scriptures are the word of God we have only the testimony of men long dead whose identity is not clearly established and who are not known to have been sworn in any sense. Under the rules of evidence as they now exist in this country, no single assertion in the Bible has in its support any evidence admissible in a court of law. It cannot be proved that the battle of Blenheim ever was fought, that there was such a person as Julius Caesar, such an empire as Assyria.

But as records of courts of justice are admissible, it can easily be proved that powerful and malevolent magicians once existed and were a scourge to mankind. The evidence (including confession) upon which certain women were convicted of witchcraft and executed was without a flaw; it is still unimpeachable. The judges' decisions based on it were sound in logic and in law. Nothing in any existing court was ever more thoroughly proved than the charges of witchcraft and sorcery for which so many suffered death. If there were no witches, human testimony and human reason are alike destitute of value.

INAUSPICIOUSLY, *adv.*
In an unpromising manner, the auspices being unfavorable. Among the Romans it was customary before undertaking any important action or enterprise to obtain from the augurs, or state prophets, some hint of its probable outcome; and one of their favorite and most trustworthy modes of divination consisted in observing the flight of birds—the omens thence derived being called *auspices.* Newspaper reporters and certain miscreant lexicographers have decided that the word—always in the plural—shall mean "patronage" or "management"; as, "The festivities were under the auspices of the Ancient and Honorable Order of Body-Snatchers"; or, "The hilarities were auspicated by the Knights of Hunger."

INCOME, *n.*
The natural and rational gauge and measure of respectability, the commonly accepted standards being artificial, arbitrary and fallacious; for, as "Sir Sycophas Chrysolater" in the play has justly remarked, "the true use and function of property (in whatsoever it consisteth—coins, or land, or houses, or merchant-stuff, or anything which may be named as holden of right to one's own subservience) as also of honors, titles, preferments and place, and all favor and acquaintance of persons of quality or ableness, are but to get money. Hence it followeth that all things are truly to be rated as of worth in measure of their serviceableness to that end; and their possessors should take rank in agreement thereto, neither the lord of an unproducing manor, howsoever broad and ancient, nor he who bears an unremunerate dignity, nor yet the pauper favorite of a king, being esteemed of level excellency with him whose riches are of daily accretion; and hardly should they whose wealth is barren claim and rightly take more honor than the poor and unworthy."

INCOMPATIBILITY, *n.*
In matrimony a similarity of tastes, particularly the taste for domination. Incompatibility may, however, consist of a meek-eyed matron living just around the corner. It has even been known to wear a moustache.

INCOMPOSSIBLE, *adj.*
Unable to exist if something else exists. Two things are incompossible when the world of being has scope enough for one of them, but not enough for both—as Walt Whitman's poetry and God's mercy to man. Incompossibility, it will be seen, is only incompatibility let loose. Instead of such low language as "Go heel yourself—I mean to kill you on sight," the words, "Sir, we are incompossible," would convey an equally significant intimation and in stately courtesy are altogether superior.

INCUBUS, *n.*
One of a race of highly improper demons who, though probably not wholly extinct, may be said to have seen their best nights. For a complete account of *incubi* and *succubi*, including *incubae*, and *succubae*, see the *Liber Demonorum* of Protassus (Paris, 1328), which contains much curious information that would be out of place in a dictionary intended as a text-book for the public schools.

Victor Hugo relates that in the Channel Islands Satan himself—tempted more than elsewhere by the beauty of the women, doubtless—sometimes plays at *incubus*, greatly to the inconvenience and alarm of the good dames who wish to be loyal to their marriage vows, generally speaking. A certain lady applied to the parish priest to learn how they might, in the dark, distinguish the hardy intruder from their husbands. The holy man said they must feel his brow for horns; but Hugo is ungallant enough to hint a doubt of the efficacy of the test.

INCUMBENT, *n.*
A person of the liveliest interest to the outcumbents.

INDECISION, *n.*
The chief element of success; "for whereas," saith Sir Thomas Brewbold, "there is but one way to do nothing and divers ways to do something, whereof, to a surety, only one is the right way, it followeth that he who from indecision standeth still hath not so many chances of going astray as he who pusheth forwards"—a most clear and satisfactory exposition of the matter.

"Your prompt decision to attack," said General Grant on a certain occasion to General Gordon Granger, "was admirable; you had but five minutes to make up your mind in."

"Yes, sir," answered the victorious subordinate, "it is a great thing to know exactly what to do in an emergency. When in doubt whether to attack or retreat I never hesitate a moment—I toss up a copper."

"Do you mean to say that's what you did this time?"

"Yes, General; but for Heaven's sake don't reprimand me: I disobeyed the coin."

INDIFFERENT, *adj.*
Imperfectly sensible to distinctions among things.

> "You tiresome man!" cried
>   Indolentio's wife,
> "You've grown indifferent to all in
>   life."
> "Indifferent?" he drawled with a
>   slow smile;
> "I would be, dear, but it is not worth
>   while."
>   *Apuleius M. Gokul.*

INDIGESTION, *n.*
A disease which the patient and his friends frequently mistake for deep religious conviction and concern for the salvation of mankind. As the simple Red Man of the western wild put it, with, it must be confessed, a certain force: "Plenty well, no pray; big bellyache, heap God."

INDIGESTION

INDISCRETION, *n.*
The guilt of woman.

INEXPEDIENT, *adj.*
Not calculated to advance one's
interests.

INFANCY, *n.*
The period of our lives when,
according to Wordsworth, "Heaven
lies about us." The world begins
lying about us pretty soon
afterward.

INFERIAE, *n.*
(Latin.) Among the Greeks and
Romans, sacrifices for propitiation
of the *Dii Manes,* or souls of dead
heroes; for the pious ancients could
not invent enough gods to satisfy
their spiritual needs, and had to
have a number of makeshift deities,
or, as a sailor might say, jury-gods,
which they made out of the most
unpromising materials. It was
while sacrificing a bullock to the
spirit of Agamemnon that Laiaides,
a priest of Aulis, was favored with
an audience of that illustrious
warrior's shade, who prophetically
recounted to him the birth of Christ
and the triumph of Christianity,
giving him also a rapid but
tolerably complete review of events
down to the reign of Saint Louis.
The narrative ended abruptly at
that point, owing to the
inconsiderate crowing of a cock,
which compelled the ghosted King
of Men to scamper back to Hades.
There is a fine mediaeval flavor to
this story, and as it has not been
traced back further than Père
Brateille, a pious but obscure
writer at the court of Saint Louis,
we shall probably not err on the
side of presumption in considering
it apocryphal, though Monsignor
Capel's judgment of the matter
might be different; and to that I
bow — wow.

INFIDEL, *n.*
In New York, one who does not
believe in the Christian religion; in
Constantinople, one who does.
A kind of scoundrel
imperfectly reverent of, and
niggardly contributory to, divines,
ecclesiastics, popes, parsons, canons,
monks, mollahs, voodoos,
presbyters, hierophants, prelates,
obeah-men, abbés, nuns,
missionaries, exhorters, deacons,
friars, hadjis, high-priests,
muezzins, brahmins, medicine-men,
confessors, eminences, elders,
primates, prebendaries, pilgrims,
prophets, imaums, beneficiaries,
clerks, vicars-choral, archbishops,
bishops, abbots, priors, preachers,
padres, abbotesses, caloyers,
palmers, curates, patriarchs,
bonzes, santons, beadsmen,
canonesses, residentiaries,
diocesans, deans, subdeans, rural
deans, abdals, charm-sellers,
archdeacons, hierarchs, class-
leaders. incumbents, capitulars,
sheiks, talapoins, postulants,
scribes, gooroos, precentors,
beadles, fakeers, sextons,
reverences, revivalists, cenobites,
perpetual curates, chaplains,
mudjoes, readers, novices, vicars,
pastors, rabbis, ulemas, lamas,
sacristans, vergers, dervises,
lectors, church wardens, cardinals,
prioresses, suffragans, acolytes,
rectors, curés, sophis, mutifs and
pumpums.

INFLUENCE, *n.*
In politics, a visionary *quo* given in
exchange for a substantial *quid.*

INGRATE, *n.*
One who receives a benefit from
another, or is otherwise an object of
charity.

"All men are ingrates," sneered the
    cynic. "Nay,"
    The good philanthropist replied;

"I did great service to a man one
    day
Who never since has cursed me to
    repay,
    Nor vilified."

"Ho!" cried the cynic, "lead me to
        him straight—
    With veneration I am overcome,
And fain would have his blessing."
    "Sad your fate—
He cannot bless you, for I grieve to
    state
    The man is dumb."
                                    Ariel Selp.

INJURY, *n.*
An offense next in degree of
enormity to a slight.

INJUSTICE, *n.*
A burden which of all those that we
load upon others and carry
ourselves is lightest in the hands
and heaviest upon the back.

INK, *n.*
A villainous compound of
tannogallate of iron, gum-arabic
and water, chiefly used to facilitate
the infection of idiocy and promote
intellectual crime. The properties of
ink are peculiar and contradictory:
it may be used to make reputations
and unmake them; to blacken them
and to make them white; but it is
most generally and acceptably
employed as a mortar to bind
together the stones in an edifice of
fame, and as a whitewash to
conceal afterward the rascal quality
of the material. There are men
called journalists who have
established ink baths which some
persons pay money to get into,
others to get out of. Not
infrequently it occurs that a person
who has paid to get in pays twice as
much to get out.

INNATE, *adj.*
Natural, inherent—as innate ideas,
that is to say, ideas that we are
born with, having had them
previously imparted to us. The
doctrine of innate ideas is one of the

INK

most admirable faiths of
philosophy, being itself an innate
idea and therefore inaccessible to
disproof, though Locke foolishly
supposed himself to have given it "a
black eye." Among innate ideas
may be mentioned the belief in
one's ability to conduct a
newspaper, in the greatness of one's
country, in the superiority of one's
civilization, in the importance of
one's personal affairs and in the
interesting nature of one's diseases.

IN'ARDS, *n.*
The stomach, heart, soul and other
bowels. Many eminent investigators
do not class the soul as an in'ard,
but that acute observer and
renowned authority, Dr. Gunsaulus,
is persuaded that the mysterious
organ known as the spleen is
nothing less than our immortal
part. To the contrary, Professor
Garrett P. Servis holds that man's
soul is that prolongation of his
spinal marrow which forms the
pith of his no tail; and for
demonstration of his faith points
confidently to the fact that tailed
animals have no souls. Concerning
these two theories, it is best to
suspend judgment by believing
both.

INSCRIPTION, *n.*
Something written on another
thing. Inscriptions are of many
kinds, but mostly memorial,
intended to commemorate the fame
of some illustrious person and hand
down to distant ages the record of
his services and virtues. To this
class of inscriptions belongs the
name of John Smith, penciled on
the Washington monument.
Following are examples of
memorial inscriptions on
tombstones:

"In the sky my soul is found,
And my body in the ground.
By and by my body'll rise
To my spirit in the skies,
Soaring up to Heaven's gate.
      1878."

"Sacred to the memory of Jeremiah
Tree. Cut down May 9th, 1862, aged 27
yrs. 4 mos. and 12 ds. Indigenous."

"Affliction sore long time she boar,
  Phisicians was in vain,
Till Deth released the dear
    deceased
  And left her a remain.
Gone to join Ananias in the regions of
  bliss."

"The clay that rests beneath this
    stone
As Silas Wood was widely known.
Now, lying here, I ask what good
It was to me to be S. Wood.
O Man, let not ambition trouble you,
Is the advice of Silas W."

INSECTIVORA, *n.*

"See," cries the chorus of admiring
  preachers,
"How Providence provides for all
  His creatures!"
"His care," the gnat said, "even the
  insects follows:
For us He has provided wrens and
  swallows."
            Sempen Railey.

INSURANCE, *n.*
An ingenious modern game of
chance in which the player is
permitted to enjoy the comfortable
conviction that he is beating the
man who keeps the table.

INSURANCE AGENT: My dear sir, that
is a fine house—pray let me insure it.

HOUSE OWNER: With pleasure. Please
make the annual premium so low that by
the time when, according to the tables of
your actuary, it will probably be
destroyed by fire I will have paid you
considerably less than the face of the
policy.

INSURANCE AGENT: O dear, no—we
could not afford to do that. We must fix
the premium so that you will have paid
more.

HOUSE OWNER: How, then, can *I*
afford *that?*

INSURANCE AGENT: Why, your house
may burn down at any time. There was
Smith's house, for example, which—

HOUSE OWNER: Spare me—there
were Brown's house, on the contrary,

INSCRIPTION

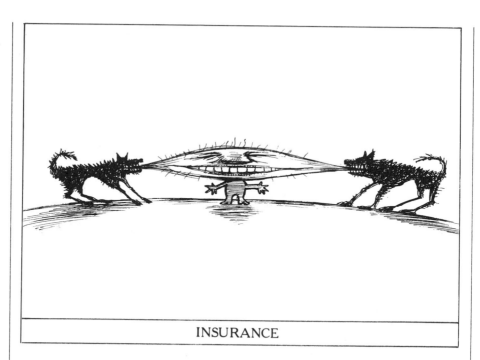

INSURANCE

and Jones's house, and Robinson's house, which—

INSURANCE AGENT: Spare *me*!

HOUSE OWNER: Let us understand each other. You want me to pay you money on the supposition that something will occur previously to the time set by yourself for its occurrence. In other words, you expect me to bet that my house will not last so long as you say that it will probably last.

INSURANCE AGENT: But if your house burns without insurance it will be a total loss.

HOUSE OWNER: Beg your pardon—by your own actuary's tables I shall probably have saved, when it burns, all the premiums I would otherwise have paid to you—amounting to more than the face of the policy they would have bought. But suppose it to burn, uninsured, before the time upon which your figures are based. If I could not afford that, how could you if it were insured?

INSURANCE AGENT: O, we should make ourselves whole from our luckier ventures with other clients. Virtually, they pay your loss.

HOUSE OWNER: And virtually, then don't I help to pay their losses? Are not,

their houses as likely as mine to burn before they have paid you as much as you must pay them? The case stands this way: you expect to take more money from your clients than you pay to them, do you not?

INSURANCE AGENT: Certainly; if we did not—

HOUSE OWNER: I would not trust you with my money. Very well, then. If it is *certain*, with reference to the whole body of your clients, that they lose money on you it is *probable*, with reference to any one of them, that *he* will. It is these individual probabilities that make the aggregate certainty.

INSURANCE AGENT: I will not deny it—but look at the figures in this pamph—

HOUSE OWNER: Heaven forbid!

INSURANCE AGENT: You spoke of saving the premiums which you would otherwise pay to me. Will you not be more likely to squander them? We offer you an incentive to thrift.

HOUSE OWNER: The willingness of A to take care of B's money is not peculiar to insurance, but as a charitable institution you command esteem. Deign to accept its expression from a Deserving Object.

INSURRECTION, *n.*
An unsuccessful revolution.
Disaffection's failure to substitute
misrule for bad government.

INTENTION, *n.*
The mind's sense of the prevalence
of one set of influences over another
set; an effect whose cause is the
imminence, immediate or remote,
of the performance of an
involuntary act.

INTERPRETER, *n.*
One who enables two persons of
different languages to understand
each other by repeating to each
what it would have been to the
interpreter's advantage for the
other to have said.

INTERREGNUM, *n.*
The period during which a
monarchical country is governed by
a warm spot on the cushion of the
throne. The experiment of letting
the spot grow cold has commonly
been attended by most unhappy
results from the zeal of many
worthy persons to make it warm
again.

INTIMACY, *n.*
A relation into which fools are
providentially drawn for their
mutual destruction.

> Two Seidlitz powders, one in blue
> And one in white, together drew,
> And having each a pleasant sense
> Of t'other powder's excellence,
> Forsook their jackets for the snug
> Enjoyment of a common mug.
> So close their intimacy grew
> One paper would have held the two.
> To confidences straight they fell,
> Less anxious each to hear than tell;
> Then each remorsefully confessed
> To all the virtues he possessed,
> Acknowledging he had them in
> So high degree it was a sin.
> The more they said, the more they
>   felt
> Their spirits with emotion melt,
> Till tears of sentiment expressed
> Their feelings. Then they
>   effervesced!
> So Nature executes her feats
> Of wrath on friends and
>   sympathetes
> The good old rule who won't apply,
> That you are you and I am I.

INTRODUCTION, *n.*
A social ceremony invented by the
devil for the gratification of his
servants and the plaguing of his
enemies. The introduction attains
its most malevolent development in
this country, being, indeed, closely
related to our political system.
Every American being the equal of
every other American, it follows
that everybody has the right to
know everybody else, which implies
the right to introduce without
request or permission. The
Declaration of Independence should
have read thus:

> "We hold these truths to be self-
> evident: that all men are created equal;
> that they are endowed by their Creator
> with certain inalienable rights; that
> among these are life, and the right to
> make that of another miserable by
> thrusting upon him an incalculable
> quantity of acquaintances; liberty,
> particularly the liberty to introduce
> persons to one another without first
> ascertaining if they are not already
> acquainted as enemies; and the pursuit
> of another's happiness with a running
> pack of strangers."

INVENTOR, *n.*
A person who makes an ingenious
arrangement of wheels, levers and
springs, and believes it civilization.

IRRELIGION, *n.*
The principal one of the great
faiths of the world.

ITCH, *n.*
The patriotism of a Scotchman.

INTERPRETER

J

J
is a consonant in English, but some nations use it as a vowel—than which nothing could be more absurd. Its original form, which has been but slightly modified, was that of the tail of a subdued dog, and it was not a letter but a character, standing for a Latin verb, *jacere*, "to throw," because when a stone is thrown at a dog the dog's tail assumes that shape. This is the origin of the letter, as expounded by the renowned Dr. Jocolpus Bumer, of the University of Belgrade, who established his conclusions on the subject in a work of three quarto volumes and committed suicide on being reminded that the j in the Roman alphabet had originally no curl.

JEALOUS, *adj.*
Unduly concerned about the preservation of that which can be lost only if not worth keeping.

JESTER, *n.*
An officer formerly attached to a king's household, whose business it was to amuse the court by ludicrous actions and utterances, the absurdity being attested by his motley costume. The king himself being attired with dignity, it took the world some centuries to discover that his own conduct and decrees were sufficiently ridiculous for the amusement not only of his court but of all mankind. The jester was commonly called a fool, but the poets and romancers have ever delighted to represent him as a singularly wise and witty person. In the circus of to-day the melancholy ghost of the court fool effects the dejection of humbler audiences with the same jests wherewith in life he gloomed the marble hall, panged the patrician sense of humor and tapped the tank of royal tears.

> The widow-queen of Portugal
>   Had an audacious jester
> Who entered the confessional
>   Disguised, and there confessed her.

> "Father," she said, "thine ear bend
>   down—
> My sins are more than scarlet:
> I love my fool—blaspheming clown,
>   And common, base-born varlet."

> "Daughter," the mimic priest
>   replied,
> "That sin, indeed, is awful:
> The church's pardon is denied
>   To love that is unlawful.

> "But since thy stubborn heart will
>   be
>   For him forever pleading,
> Thou'dst better make him, by
>   decree,
>   A man of birth and breeding."

> She made the fool a duke, in hope
>   With Heaven's taboo to palter;
> Then told a priest, who told the
>   Pope,
>   Who damned her from the altar!
>   *Barel Dort.*

JUSTICE, *n.*
A commodity which in a more or less adulterated condition the State sells to the citizen as a reward for his allegiance, taxes and personal service.

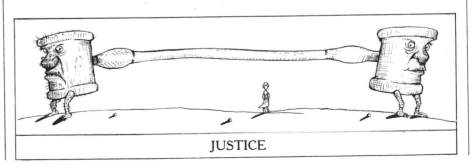

JUSTICE

K

K
is a consonant that we get from the Greeks, but it can be traced away back beyond them to the Cerathians, a small commercial nation inhabiting the peninsula of Smero. In their tongue it was called *Klatch*, which means "destroyed." The form of the letter was originally precisely that of our H, but the erudite Dr. Snedeker explains that it was altered to its present shape to commemorate the destruction of the great temple of Jarute by an earthquake, *circa* 730 B. C. This building was famous for the two lofty columns of its portico, one of which was broken in half by the catastrophe, the other remaining intact. As the earlier form of the letter is supposed to have been suggested by these pillars, so, it is thought by the great antiquary, its later was adopted as a simple and natural—not to say touching—means of keeping the calamity ever in the national memory. It is not known if the name of the letter was altered as an additional mnemonic, or if the name was always *Klatch* and the destruction one of nature's puns. As each theory seems probable enough, I see no objection to believing both—and Dr. Snedeker arrayed himself on that side of the question.

KEEP, *v. t.*

He willed away his whole estate,
  And then in death he fell asleep,
Murmuring: "Well, at any rate,
  My name unblemished I shall
    keep."
But when upon the tomb 'twas
    wrought
Whose was it?—for the dead keep
    naught.
  Durang Gophel Arn.

KILL, *v. t.*
To create a vacancy without nominating a successor.

KILT, *n.*
A costume sometimes worn by Scotchmen in America and Americans in Scotland.

KINDNESS, *n.*
A brief preface to ten volumes of exaction.

KING, *n.*
A male person commonly known in America as a "crowned head," although he never wears a crown and has usually no head to speak of.

A king, in times long, long gone by,
  Said to his lazy jester:
"If I were you and you were I
My moments merrily would fly—
  No care nor grief to pester."

"The reason, Sire, that you would
    thrive,"
  The fool said—"if you'll hear it—
Is that of all the fools alive
Who own you for their sovereign,
    I've
  The most forgiving spirit."
    Oogum Bem.

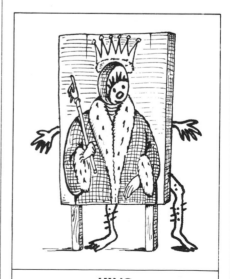

KING

65

KING'S EVIL, *n.*
A malady that was formerly cured
by the touch of the sovereign, but
has now to be treated by the
physicians. Thus "the most pious
Edward" of England used to lay his
royal hand upon his ailing subjects
and make them whole—

> a crowd of wretched souls
> That stay his cure: their malady
> convinces
> The great essay of art; but at his
> touch,
> Such sanctity hath Heaven given his
> hand,
> They presently amend,

as the "Doctor" in *Macbeth* hath it.
This useful property of the royal hand
could, it appears, be transmitted
along with other crown properties;
for according to "Malcolm,"

> 'tis spoken,
> To the succeeding royalty he leaves
> The healing benediction.

But the gift somewhere dropped
out of the line of succession: the later
sovereigns of England have not been
tactual healers, and the disease once
honored with the name "king's evil"
now bears the humble one of
"scrofula," from *scrofa*, a sow. The
date and author of the following
epigram are known only to the author
of this dictionary, but it is old enough
to show that the jest about Scotland's
national disorder is not a thing of
yesterday.

> Ye Kynge his evil in me laye,
> Wh. he of Scottlande charmed
> awaye.
> He layde his hand on mine and sayd:
> "Be gone!" Ye ill no longer stayd.
> But O ye wofull plyght in wh.
> I'm now y-pight: I have ye itche!

The superstition that maladies can
be cured by royal taction is dead, but
like many a departed conviction it has
left a monument of custom to keep its
memory green. The practice of
forming in line and shaking the
President's hand had no other origin,
and when that great dignitary
bestows his healing salutation on

> strangely visited people,
> All swoln and ulcerous, pitiful to the
> eye,
> The mere despair of surgery,

he and his patients are handing along
an extinguished torch which once
was kindled at the altar-fire of a faith
long held by all classes of men. It is a
beautiful and edifying "survival"—
one which brings the sainted past
close home to our "business and
bosoms."

KISS, *n.*
A word invented by the poets as a
rhyme for "bliss." It is supposed to
signify, in a general way, some kind
of rite or ceremony appertaining to
a good understanding; but the
manner of its performance is
unknown to this lexicographer.

KLEPTOMANIAC, *n.*
A rich thief.

KNIGHT, *n.*

> Once a warrior gentle of birth,
> Then a person of civic worth,
> Now a fellow to move our mirth.
> Warrior, person, and fellow—no
> more:
> We must knight our dogs to get any
> lower.
> Brave Knights Kennelers then shall
> be,
> Noble Knights of the Golden Flea,
> Knights of the Order of St. Steboy,
> Knights of St. Gorge and Sir
> Knights Jawy.
> God speed the day when this
> knighting fad
> Shall go to the dogs and the dogs go
> mad.

KORAN, *n.*
A book which the Mohammedans
foolishly believe to have been
written by divine inspiration, but
which Christians know to be a
wicked imposture, contradictory to
the Holy Scriptures.

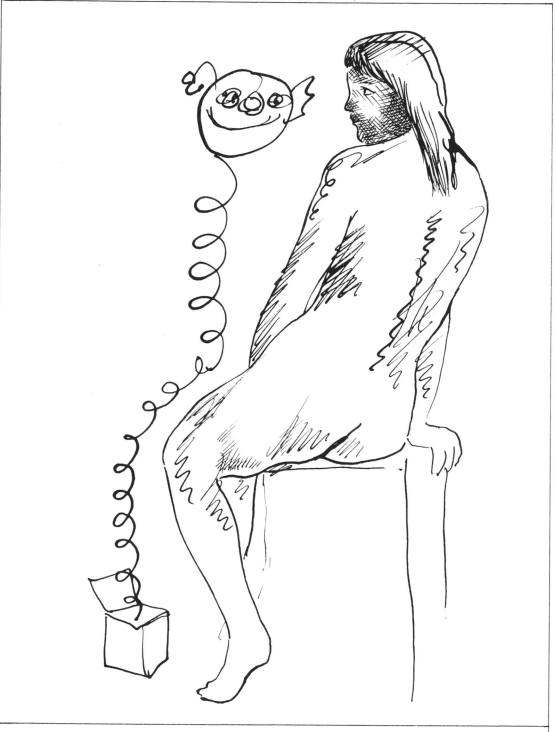

KISS

L

LABOR, *n.*
One of the processes by which A acquires property for B.

LAND, *n.*
A part of the earth's surface, considered as property. The theory that land is property subject to private ownership and control is the foundation of modern society, and is eminently worthy of the superstructure. Carried to its logical conclusion, it means that some have the right to prevent others from living; for the right to own implies the right exclusively to occupy; and in fact laws of trespass are enacted wherever property in land is recognized. It follows that if the whole area of *terra firma* is owned by A, B and C, there will be no place for D, E, F and G to be born, or, born as trespassers, to exist.

> A life on the ocean wave,
> A home on the rolling deep,
> For the spark that nature gave
> I have there the right to keep.
>
> They give me the cat-o'-nine
> Whenever I go ashore.
> Then ho! for the flashing brine —
> I'm a natural commodore!
> *Dodle.*

LANGUAGE, *n.*
The music with which we charm the serpents guarding another's treasure.

LAOCOON, *n.*
A famous piece of antique sculpture representing a priest of that name and his two sons in the folds of two enormous serpents. The skill and diligence with which the old man and lads support the serpents and keep them up to their work have been justly regarded as one of the noblest artistic illustrations of the mastery of human intelligence over brute inertia.

LAUGHTER, *n.*
An interior convulsion, producing a distortion of the features and accompanied by inarticulate noises. It is infectious and, though intermittent, incurable. Liability to attacks of laughter is one of the characteristics distinguishing man from the animals — these being not only inaccessible to the provocation of his example, but impregnable to the microbes having original jurisdiction in bestowal of the disease. Whether laughter could be imparted to animals by inoculation from the human patient is a question that has not been answered by experimentation. Dr. Meir Witchell holds that the infectious character of laughter is due to instantaneous fermentation of *sputa* diffused in a spray. From this peculiarity he names the disorder *Convulsio spargens.*

LAUREATE, *adj.*
Crowned with leaves of the laurel. In England the Poet Laureate is an officer of the sovereign's court, acting as dancing skeleton at every royal feast and singing-mute at every royal funeral. Of all incumbents of that high office, Robert Southey had the most notable knack at drugging the Samson of public joy and cutting his hair to the quick; and he had an artistic color-sense which enabled him so to blacken a public grief as to give it the aspect of a national crime.

LAUREL, *n.*
The *laurus,* a vegetable dedicated to Apollo, and formerly defoliated to wreathe the brows of victors and such poets as had influence at court. (*Vide supra.*)

LAWYER, *n.*
One skilled in circumvention of the law.

LAWYER

LAZINESS, n.
Unwarranted repose of manner in a person of low degree.

LEAD, n.
A heavy blue-gray metal much used in giving stability to light lovers — particularly to those who love not wisely but other men's wives. Lead is also of great service as a counterpoise to an argument of such weight that it turns the scale of debate the wrong way. An interesting fact in the chemistry of international controversy is that at the point of contact of two patriotisms lead is precipitated in great quantities.

> Hail, holy Lead! — of human feuds the
>   great
>   And universal arbiter; endowed
> With penetration to pierce any cloud
> Fogging the field of controversial hate,
> And with a swift, inevitable, straight,
>   Searching precision find the
>   unavowed
>   But vital point. Thy judgment, when
>   allowed
> By the chirurgeon, settles the debate.
> O useful metal! — were it not for thee
>   We'd grapple one another's ears
>   alway:
> But when we hear thee buzzing like a
>   bee
>   We, like old Muhlenberg, "care not
>   to stay."
> And when the quick have run away
>   like pullets
> Jack Satan smelts the dead to make
>   new bullets.

LEARNING, n.
The kind of ignorance distinguishing the studious.

LECTURER, n.
One with his hand in your pocket, his tongue in your ear and his faith in your patience.

LEGACY, n.
A gift from one who is legging it out of this vale of tears.

LEONINE, adj.
Unlike a menagerie lion. Leonine verses are those in which a word in the middle of a line rhymes with a word at the end, as in this famous passage from Bella Peeler Silcox:

> The electric light invades the dunnest
>   deep of Hades.
> Cries Pluto,'twixt his snores: "O
>   tempora! O mores!"

It should be explained that Mrs. Silcox does not undertake to teach the pronunciation of the Greek and Latin tongues. Leonine verses are so called in honor of a poet named Leo, whom prosodists appear to find a pleasure in believing to have been the first to discover that a rhyming couplet could be run into a single line.

LETTUCE, n.
An herb of the genus *Lactuca*, "Wherewith," says that pious gastronome, Hengist Pelly, "God has been pleased to reward the good and punish the wicked. For by his inner light the righteous man has discerned a manner of compounding for it a dressing to the appetency whereof a multitude of gustible condiments conspire, being reconciled and ameliorated with profusion of oil, the entire comestible making glad the heart of the godly and causing his face to shine. But the person of spiritual unworth is successfully tempted of the Adversary to eat of lettuce with destitution of oil, mustard, egg, salt and garlic, and with a rascal bath of vinegar polluted with sugar. Wherefore the person of spiritual unworth suffers an intestinal pang of strange complexity and raises the song."

LEVIATHAN, n.
An enormous aquatic animal mentioned by Job. Some suppose it to have been the whale, but that distinguished ichthyologer, Dr. Jordan, of Stanford University, maintains with considerable heat that it was a species of gigantic

Tadpole (*Thaddeus Polandensis*) or Polliwig—*Maria pseudo-hirsuta*. For an exhaustive description and history of the Tadpole consult the famous monograph of Jane Porter, *Thaddeus of Warsaw.*

LEXICOGRAPHER, *n.*
A pestilent fellow, who, under the pretense of recording some particular stage in the development of a language, does what he can to arrest its growth, stiffen its flexibility and mechanize its methods. For your lexicographer, having written his dictionary, comes to be considered "as one having authority," whereas his function is only to make a record, not to give a law. The natural servility of the human understanding having invested him with judicial power, surrenders its right of reason and sumbits itself to a chronicle as if it were a statute. Let the dictionary (for example) mark a good word as "obsolete" or "obsolescent" and few men thereafter venture to use it, whatever their need of it and however desirable its restoration to favor—whereby the process of impoverishment is accelerated and speech decays. On the contrary, the bold and discerning writer who, recognizing the truth that language must grow by innovation if it grow at all, makes new words and uses the old in an unfamiliar sense, has no following and is tartly reminded that "it isn't in the dictionary"— although down to the time of the first lexicographer (Heaven forgive him!) no author ever had used a word that *was* in the dictionary. In the golden prime and high noon of English speech; when from the lips of the great Elizabethans fell words that made their own meaning and carried it in their very sound; when a Shakespeare and a Bacon were possible, and the language now rapidly perishing at one end and slowly renewed at the other was in vigorous growth and hardy preservation—sweeter than honey and stronger than a lion—the lexicographer was a person unknown, the dictionary a creation which his Creator had not created him to create.

> God said: "Let Spirit perish into Form,"
> And lexicographers arose, a swarm!
> Thought fled and left her clothing, which they took,
> And catalogued each garment in a book.
> Now, from her leafy covert when she cries:
> "Give me my clothes and I'll return," they rise
> And scan the list, and say without compassion:
> "Excuse us—they are mostly out of fashion."
>
> *Sigismund Smith.*

LIAR, *n.*
A lawyer with a roving commission.

LIBERTY, *n.*
One of Imagination's most precious possessions.

LIBERTY

LICKSPITTLE, *n.*
A useful functionary, not
infrequently found editing a
newspaper. In his character of
editor he is closely allied to the
blackmailer by the tie of occasional
identity; for in truth the lickspittle
is only the blackmailer under
another aspect, though the latter is
frequently found as an independent
species. Lickspittling is more
detestable than blackmailing,
precisely as the business of a
confidence man is more detestable
than that of a highway robber; and
the parallel maintains itself
throughout, for whereas few
robbers will cheat, every sneak will
plunder if he dare.

LIFE, *n.*
A spiritual pickle preserving the
body from decay. We live in daily
apprehension of its loss; yet when
lost it is not missed. The question,
"Is life worth living?" has been
much discussed; particularly by
those who think it is not, many of
whom have written at great length
in support of their view and by
careful observance of the laws of
health enjoyed for long terms of
years the honors of successful
controversy.

> "Life's not worth living, and that's
>   the truth,"
> Carelessly caroled the golden youth.
> In manhood still he maintained that
>   view
> And held it more strongly the older
>   he grew.
> When kicked by a jackass at eighty-
>   three,
> "Go fetch me a surgeon at once!"
>   cried he.
>
> *Han Soper.*

LIGHTHOUSE, *n.*
A tall building on the seashore in
which the government maintains a
lamp and the friend of a politician.

LIMB, *n.*
The branch of a tree or the leg of
an American woman.

LINEN, *n.*
"A kind of cloth the making of
which, when made of hemp, entails
a great waste of hemp."—*Calcraft
the Hangman.*

LITIGANT, *n.*
A person about to give up his skin
for the hope of retaining his bones.

LITIGATION, *n.*
A machine which you go into as a
pig and come out as a sausage.

LIVER, *n.*
A large red organ thoughtfully
provided by nature to be bilious
with. The sentiments and emotions
which every literary anatomist now
knows to haunt the heart were
anciently believed to infest the
liver; and even Gascoygne, speaking
of the emotional side of human
nature, calls it "our hepaticall
parte." It was at one time
considered the seat of life; hence its
name—liver, the thing we live
with. The liver is heaven's best gift
to the goose; without it that bird
would be unable to supply us with
the Strasbourg *pâté.*

LL.D.
Letters indicating the degree
Legumptionorum Doctor, one
learned in laws, gifted with legal
gumption. Some suspicion is cast
upon this derivation by the fact that
the title was formerly LL.d., and
conferred only upon gentlemen
distinguished for their wealth. At
the date of this writing Columbia
University is considering the
expediency of making another
degree for clergymen, in place of
the old D.D.—*Damnator Diaboli.*
The new honor will be known as
Sanctorum Custus, and written $$c.

LIFE

LOCK-AND-KEY, *n.*
The distinguishing device of
civilization and enlightenment.

LODGER, *n.*
A less popular name for the Second
Person of that delectable newspaper
Trinity, the Roomer, the Bedder
and the Mealer.

LOGIC, *n.*
The art of thinking and reasoning
in strict accordance with the
limitations and incapacities of the
human misunderstanding. The
basic of logic is the syllogism,
consisting of a major and a minor
premise and a conclusion—thus:

> *Major Premise*: Sixty men can do a
> piece of work sixty times as
> quickly as one man.
> *Minor Premise*: One man can dig a
> posthole in sixty seconds;
> therefore—
> *Conclusion*: Sixty men can dig a
> posthole in one second.

LOGOMACHY, *n.*
A war in which the weapons are
words and the wounds punctures in
the swim-bladder of self-esteem—a
kind of contest in which, the
vanquished being unconscious of
defeat, the victor is denied the
reward of success.

> 'Tis said by divers of the scholar-
> men
> That poor Salmasius died of Milton's
> pen.
> Alas! we cannot know if this is true,
> For reading Milton's wit we perish
> too.

LONGANIMITY, *n.*
The disposition to endure injury
with meek forbearance while
maturing a plan of revenge.

LONGEVITY, *n.*
Uncommon extension of the fear of
death.

LOOKING-GLASS, *n.*
A vitreous plane upon which to
display a fleeting show for man's
disillusion given.

The King of Manchuria had a
magic looking-glass, whereon whoso
looked saw, not his own image, but
only that of the king. A certain
courtier who had long enjoyed the
king's favor and was thereby
enriched beyond any other subject
of the realm, said to the king: "Give
me, I pray, thy wonderful mirror,
so that when absent out of thine
august presence I may yet do
homage before thy visible shadow,
prostrating myself night and
morning in the glory of thy benign
countenance, as which nothing has
so divine splendor, O Noonday Sun
of the Universe!"

Pleased with the speech, the king
commanded that the mirror be
conveyed to the courtier's palace;
but after, having gone thither
without apprisal, he found it in an
apartment where was naught but
idle lumber. And the mirror was
dimmed with dust and overlaced
with cobwebs. This so angered him
that he fisted it hard, shattering the
glass, and was sorely hurt. Enraged
all the more by this mischance, he
commanded that the ungrateful
courtier be thrown into prison, and
that the glass be repaired and
taken back to his own palace; and
this was done. But when the king
looked again on the mirror he saw
not his image as before, but only
the figure of a crowned ass, having
a bloody bandage on one of its
hinder hooves—as the artificers
and all who had looked upon it had
before discerned but feared to
report. Taught wisdom and charity,
the king restored his courtier to
liberty, had the mirror set into the
back of the throne and reigned
many years with justice and
humility; and one day when he fell
asleep in death while on the throne,
the whole court saw in the mirror
the luminous figure of an angel,
which remains to this day.

LONGEVITY

LOQUACITY, *n.*
A disorder which renders the
sufferer unable to curb his tongue
when you wish to talk.

LORD, *n.*
In American society, an English
tourist above the state of a
costermonger, as, Lord
'Aberdasher, Lord Hartisan and so
forth. The traveling Briton of lesser
degree is addressed as "Sir," as, Sir
'Arry Donkiboi, of 'Amstead 'Eath.
The word "Lord" is sometimes used,
also, as a title of the Supreme
Being; but this is thought to be
rather flattery than true reverence.

Miss Sallie Ann Splurge, of her own
    accord,
Wedded a wandering English lord—
Wedded and took him to dwell with
    her "paw,"
A parent who throve by the practice of
    Draw.
Lord Cadde I don't hesitate here to
    declare
Unworthy the father-in-legal care
Of that elderly sport, notwithstanding
    the truth
That Cadde had renounced all the
    follies of youth;
For, sad to relate, he'd arrived at the
    stage
Of existence that's marked by the
    vices of age.
Among them, cupidity caused him to
    urge
Repeated demands on the pocket of
    Splurge,
Till, wrecked in his fortune, that
    gentleman saw
Inadequate aid in the practice of
    Draw,
And took, as a means of augmenting
    his pelf,
To the business of being a lord
    himself.
His neat-fitting garments he wilfully
    shed
And sacked himself strangely in
    checks instead;
Denuded his chin, but retained at each
    ear
A whisker that looked like a blasted
    career.
He painted his neck an incarnadine
    hue
Each morning and varnished it all
    that he knew.

The moony monocular set in his eye
Appeared to be scanning the Sweet
    Bye-and-Bye.
His head was enroofed with a
    billycock hat,
And his low-necked shoes were
    aduncous and flat.
In speech he eschewed his American
    ways,
Denying his nose to the use of his A's
And dulling their edge till the delicate
    sense
Of a babe at their temper could take
    no offence.
His H's—'twas most inexpressibly
    sweet,
The patter they made as they fell at
    his feet!
Re-outfitted thus, Mr. Splurge without
    fear
Began as Lord Splurge his recouping
    career.
Alas, the Divinity shaping his end
Entertained other views and decided
    to send
His lordship in horror, despair and
    dismay
From the land of the nobleman's
    natural prey.
For, smit with his Old World ways,
    Lady Cadde
Fell—suffering Caesar!—in love with
    her dad!
                         G. J.

LORE, *n.*
Learning—particularly that sort
which is not derived from a regular
course of instruction but comes of
the reading of occult books, or by
nature. This latter is commonly
designated as folk-lore and
embraces popularly myths and
superstitions. In Baring-Gould's
Curious Myths of the Middle Ages
the reader will find many of these
traced backward, through various
peoples on converging lines, toward
a common origin in remote
antiquity. Among these are the
fables of "Teddy the Giant Killer,"
"The Sleeping John Sharp
Williams," "Little Red Riding Hood
and the Sugar Trust," "Beauty and
the Brisbane," "The Seven
Aldermen of Ephesus," "Rip Van
Fairbanks," and so forth. The fable
which Goethe so affectingly relates
under the title of "The Erl-King"

was known two thousand years ago in Greece as "The Demos and the Infant Industry." One of the most general and ancient of these myths is that Arabian tale of "Ali Baba and the Forty Rockefellers."

LOSS, *n.*
Privation of that which we had, or had not. Thus, in the latter sense, it is said of a defeated candidate that he "lost his election"; and of that eminent man, the poet Gilder, that he has "lost his mind." It is in the former and more legitimate sense, that the word is used in the famous epitaph:

> Here Huntington's ashes long have
>   lain
> Whose loss is our own eternal gain,
> For while he exercised all his
>   powers
> Whatever he gained, the loss was
>   ours.

LOVE, *n.*
A temporary insanity curable by marriage or by removal of the patient from the influences under which he incurred the disorder. This disease, like *caries* and many other ailments, is prevalent only among civilized races living under artificial conditions; barbarous nations breathing pure air and eating simple food enjoy immunity from its ravages. It is sometimes fatal, but more frequently to the physician than to the patient.

LOW-BRED, *adj.*
"Raised" instead of brought up.

LUMINARY, *n.*
One who throws light upon a subject; as an editor by not writing about it.

LUNARIAN, *n.*
An inhabitant of the moon, as distinguished from Lunatic, one whom the moon inhabits. The Lunarians have been described by

LOVE

Lucian, Locke and other observers, but without much agreement. For example, Bragellos avers their anatomical identity with Man, but Professor Newcomb says they are more like the hill tribes of Vermont.

LYRE, *n.*
An ancient instrument of torture. The word is now used in a figurative sense to denote the poetic faculty, as in the following fiery lines of our great poet, Ella Wheeler Wilcox:

> I sit astride Parnassus with my lyre,
> And pick with care the disobedient
>   wire.
> The stupid shepherd lolling on his
>   crook
> With deaf attention scarcely deigns
>   to look.
> I bide my time, and it shall come at
>   length,
> When, with a Titan's energy and
>   strength,
> I'll grab a fistful of the strings, and
>   O,
> The world shall suffer when I let
>   them go!
>   *Farquharson Harris.*

M

MACE, *n.*
A staff of office signifying authority. Its form, that of a heavy club, indicates its original purpose and use in dissuading from dissent.

MACHINATION, *n.*
The method employed by one's opponents in baffling one's open and honorable efforts to do the right thing.

> So plain the advantages of
>   machination
> It constitutes a moral obligation,
> And honest wolves who think upon't
>   with loathing
> Feel bound to don the sheep's
>   deceptive clothing.
> So prospers still the diplomatic art,
> And Satan bows, with hand upon his
>   heart.
>   *R. S. K.*

MACROBIAN, *n.*
One forgotten of the gods and living to a great age. History is abundantly supplied with examples, from Methuselah to Old Parr, but some notable instances of longevity are less well known. A Calabrian peasant named Coloni, born in 1753, lived so long that he had what he considered a glimpse of the dawn of universal peace. Scanavius relates that he knew an archbishop who was so old that he could remember a time when he did not deserve hanging. In 1566 a linen draper of Bristol, England, declared that he had lived five hundred years, and that in all that time he had never told a lie. There are instances of longevity (*macrobiosis*) in our own country. Senator Chauncey Depew is old enough to know better. The editor of *The American,* a newspaper in New York City, has a memory that goes back to the time when he was a rascal, but not to the fact. The President of the United States was born so long ago that many of the friends of his youth have risen to high political and military preferment without the assistance of personal merit.

MAD, *adj.*
Affected with a high degree of intellectual independence; not conforming to standards of thought, speech and action derived by the conformants from study of themselves; at odds with the majority; in short, unusual. It is noteworthy that persons are pronounced mad by officials destitute of evidence that themselves are sane. For illustration, this present (and illustrious) lexicographer is no firmer in the faith of his own sanity than is any inmate of any madhouse in the land; yet for aught he knows to the contrary, instead of the lofty occupation that seems to him to be engaging his powers he may really be beating his hands against the window bars of an asylum and declaring himself Noah Webster, to the innocent delight of many thoughtless spectators.

MAGDALENE, *n.*
An inhabitant of Magdala. Popularly, a woman found out. This definition of the word has the authority of ignorance, Mary of Magdala being another person than the penitent woman mentioned by St. Luke. It has also the official sanction of the governments of Great Britain and the United States. In England the word is pronounced Maudlin, whence maudlin, adjective, unpleasantly sentimental. With their Maudlin for Magdalene, and their Bedlam for Bethlehem, the English may justly boast themselves the greatest of revisers.

MAGIC, *n.*
An art of converting superstition into coin. There are other arts serving the same high purpose, but the discreet lexicographer does not name them.

MAGNET, *n.*
Something acted upon by magnetism.

MAD

MAGNETISM, *n.*
Something acting upon a magnet.

The two definitions immediately foregoing are condensed from the works of one thousand eminent scientists, who have illuminated the subject with a great white light, to the inexpressible advancement of human knowledge.

MAGNIFICENT, *adj.*
Having a grandeur or splendor superior to that to which the spectator is accustomed, as the ears of an ass, to a rabbit, or the glory of a glowworm, to a maggot.

MAGNITUDE, *n.*
Size. Magnitude being purely relative, nothing is large and nothing small. If everything in the universe were increased in bulk one thousand diameters nothing would be any larger than it was before, but if one thing remained unchanged all the others would be larger than they had been. To an understanding familiar with the relativity of magnitude and distance the spaces and masses of the astronomer would be no more impressive than those of the microscopist. For anything we know to the contrary, the visible universe may be a small part of an atom, with its component ions, floating in the life-fluid (luminiferous ether) of some animal. Possibly the wee creatures peopling the corpuscles of our own blood are overcome with the proper emotion when contemplating the unthinkable distance from one of these to another.

MAGPIE, *n.*
A bird whose thievish disposition suggested to some one that it might be taught to talk.

MAIDEN, *n.*
A young person of the unfair sex addicted to clewless conduct and views that madden to crime. The genus has a wide geographical distribution, being found wherever sought and deplored wherever found. The maiden is not altogether unpleasing to the eye, nor (without her piano and her views) insupportable to the ear, though in respect to comeliness distinctly inferior to the rainbow, and, with regard to the part of her that is audible, beaten out of the field by the canary—which, also, is more portable.

> A lovelorn maiden she sat and
>   sang—
>   This quaint, sweet song sang she:
> "It's O for a youth with a football
>   bang
>   And a muscle fair to see!
>   The Captain he
>   Of a team to be!
> On the gridiron he shall shine,
> A monarch by right divine,
>   And never to roast on it—me!"
>   *Opoline Jones.*

MAJESTY, *n.*
The state and title of a king. Regarded with a just contempt by the Most Eminent Grand Masters, Grand Chancellors, Great Incohonees and Imperial Potentates of the ancient and honorable orders of republican America.

MALE, *n.*
A member of the unconsidered, or negligible sex. The male of the human race is commonly known (to the female) as Mere Man. The genus has two varieties: good providers and bad providers.

MALEFACTOR, *n.*
The chief factor in the progress of the human race.

MAMMALIA

MAN

MALTHUSIAN, *adj.*
Pertaining to Malthus and his
doctrines. Malthus believed in
artificially limiting population, but
found that it could not be done by
talking. One of the most practical
exponents of the Malthusian idea
was Herod of Judea, though all the
famous soldiers have been of the
same way of thinking.

MAMMALIA, *n. pl.*
A family of vertebrate animals
whose females in a state of nature
suckle their young, but when
civilized and enlightened put them
out to nurse, or use the bottle.

MAMMON, *n.*
The god of the world's leading
religion. His chief temple is in the
holy city of New York.

> He swore that all other religions were
>   gammon,
> And wore out his knees in the worship
>   of Mammon.
>   *Jared Oopf.*

MAN, *n.*
An animal so lost in rapturous
contemplation of what he thinks he
is as to overlook what he
indubitably ought to be. His chief
occupation is extermination of other
animals and his own species, which,
however, multiplies with such
insistent rapidity as to infest the
whole habitable earth and Canada.

> When the world was young and Man
>   was new,
>   And everything was pleasant,
> Distinctions Nature never drew
>   'Mongst king and priest and
>   peasant.
>   We're not that way at present,
> Save here in this Republic, where
>   We have that old régime,
> For all are kings, however bare
>   Their backs, howe'er extreme
> Their hunger. And, indeed, each has
>   a voice
> To accept the tyrant of his party's
>   choice.

A citizen who would not vote,
    And, therefore, was detested,
Was one day with a tarry coat
    (With feathers backed and
        breasted)
    By patriots invested.
"It is your duty," cried the crowd,
    "Your ballot true to cast
For the man o' your choice." He
        humbly bowed,
    And explained his wicked past;
"That's what I very gladly would
        have done,
Dear patriots, but he has never run."
                    Apperton Duke.

MANES, *n.*
The immortal parts of dead Greeks
and Romans. They were in a state
of dull discomfort until the bodies
from which they had exhaled were
buried and burned; and they seem
not to have been particularly happy
afterward.

MANICHEISM, *n.*
The ancient Persian doctrine of an
incessant warfare between Good
and Evil. When Good gave up the
fight the Persians joined the
victorious Opposition.

MANNA, *n.*
A food miraculously given to the
Israelites in the wilderness. When it
was no longer supplied to them they
settled down and tilled the soil,
fertilizing it, as a rule, with the
bodies of the original occupants.

MARRIAGE, *n.*
The state or condition of a
community consisting of a master, a
mistress and two slaves, making in
all, two.

MARTYR, *n.*
One who moves along the line of
least reluctance to a desired death.

MARRIAGE

MATERIAL, *adj.*
Having an actual existence, as
distinguished from an imaginary
one. Important.

> Material things I know, or feel, or
>   see;
> All else is immaterial to me.
>   *Jamarach Holobom.*

MAUSOLEUM, *n.*
The final and funniest folly of the
rich.

MAYONNAISE, *n.*
One of the sauces which serve the
French in place of a state religion.

ME, *pro.*
The objectionable case of I. The
personal pronoun in English has
three cases, the dominative, the
objectionable and the oppressive.
Each is all three.

MEANDER, *n.*
To proceed sinuously and aimlessly. The word is the ancient name of a river about one hundred and fifty miles south of Troy, which turned and twisted in the effort to get out of hearing when the Greeks and Trojans boasted of their prowess.

MEDAL, *n.*
A small metal disk given as a reward for virtues, attainments or services more or less authentic.

It is related of Bismark, who had been awarded a medal for gallantly rescuing a drowning person, that, being asked the meaning of the medal, he replied: "I save lives sometimes." And somctimes he didn't.

MEDICINE, *n.*
A stone flung down the Bowery to kill a dog in Broadway.

MEDICINE

MEEKNESS, *n.*
Uncommon patience in planning a revenge that is worth while.

> M is for Moses,
>   Who slew the Egyptian.
> As sweet as a rose is
> The meekness of Moses.
> No monument shows his
>   Post-mortem inscription,
> But M is for Moses,
>   Who slew the Egyptian.
> *The Biographical Alphabet.*

MEERSCHAUM, *n.*
(Literally, seafoam, and by many erroneously supposed to be made of it.) A fine white clay, which for convenience in coloring it brown is made into tobacco pipes and smoked by the workmen engaged in that industry. The purpose of coloring it has not been disclosed by the manufacturers.

> There was a youth (you've heard
>   before,
>   This woful tale, may be),
> Who bought a meerschaum pipe and
>   swore
>   That color it would be!
>
> He shut himself from the world
>   away,
>   Nor any soul he saw.
> He smoked by night, he smoked by
>   day,
>   As hard as he could draw.
>
> His dog died moaning in the wrath
>   Of winds that blew aloof;
> The weeds were in the gravel path,
>   The owl was on the roof.
>
> "He's gone afar, he'll come no more,"
>   The neighbors sadly say.
> And so they batter in the door
>   To take his goods away.
>
> Dead, pipe in mouth, the youngster
>   lay,
>   Nut-brown in face and limb.
> "That pipe's a lovely white," they
>   say,
>   "But it has colored him!"
>
> The moral there's small need to
>   sing —
>   'Tis plain as day to you:
> Don't play your game on any thing
>   That is a gamester too.
> *Martin Bulstrode.*

MENDACIOUS, *adj.*
Addicted to rhetoric.

MERCHANT, *n.*
One engaged in a commercial pursuit. A commercial pursuit is one in which the thing pursued is a dollar.

MERCY, *n.*
An attribute beloved of detected offenders.

MESMERISM, *n.*
Hypnotism before it wore good clothes, kept a carriage and asked Incredulity to dinner.

METROPOLIS, *n.*
A stronghold of provincialism.

MILLENNIUM, *n.*
The period of a thousand years when the lid is to be screwed down, with all reformers on the under side.

MIND, *n.*
A mysterious form of matter secreted by the brain. Its chief activity consists in the endeavor to ascertain its own nature, the futility of the attempt being due to the fact that it has nothing but itself to know itself with. From the Latin *mens*, a fact unknown to that honest shoe-seller, who, observing that his learned competitor over the way had displayed the motto "*Mens conscia recti,*" emblazoned his own shop front with the words "Men's, women's and children's conscia recti."

MINE, *adj.*
Belonging to me if I can hold or seize it.

MINISTER, *n.*
An agent of a higher power with a lower responsibility. In diplomacy an officer sent into a foreign country as the visible embodiment of his sovereign's hostility. His principal qualification is a degree of plausible inveracity next below that of an ambassador.

MINOR, *adj.*
Less objectionable.

MINSTREL, *adj.*
Formerly a poet, singer or musician; now a nigger with a color less than skin deep and a humor more than flesh and blood can bear.

MIRACLE, *n.*
An act or event out of the order of nature and unaccountable, as beating a normal hand of four kings and an ace with four aces and a king.

MISCREANT, *n.*
A person of the highest degree of unworth. Etymologically, the word means unbeliever, and its present signification may be regarded as theology's noblest contribution to the development of our language.

MISDEMEANOR, *n.*
An infraction of the law having less dignity than a felony and constituting no claim to admittance into the best criminal society.

By misdemeanors he essayed to climb
Into the aristocracy of crime.
O, woe was him!—with manner chill
    and grand
"Captains of industry" refused his
    hand,
"Kings of finance" denied him
    recognition
And "railway magnates" jeered his
    low condition.
He robbed a bank to make himself
    respected.
They still rebuffed him, for he was
    detected.
                S. V. Hanipur.

MIND

MISERICORDE, *n.*
A dagger which in mediaeval
warfare was used by the foot
soldier to remind an unhorsed
knight that he was mortal.

MISFORTUNE, *n.*
The kind of fortune that never
misses.

MISS, *n.*
A title with which we brand
unmarried women to indicate that
they are in the market. Miss, Missis
(Mrs.) and Mister (Mr.) are the
three most distinctly disagreeable
words in the language, in sound
and sense. Two are corruptions of
Mistress, the other of Master. In the
general abolition of social titles in
this our country they miraculously
escaped to plague us. If we must
have them let us be consistent and
give one to the unmarried man. I
venture to suggest Mush,
abbreviated to Mh.

MOLECULE, *n.*
The ultimate, indivisible unit of
matter. It is distinguished from the
corpuscle, also the ultimate,
indivisible unit of matter, by a
closer resemblance to the atom, also
the ultimate, indivisible unit of
matter. Three great scientific
theories of the structure of the
universe are the molecular, the
corpuscular and the atomic. A
fourth affirms, with Haeckel, the
condensation or precipitation of
matter from ether — whose
existence is proved by the
condensation or precipitation. The
present trend of scientific thought
is toward the theory of ions. The ion
differs from the molecule, the
corpuscle and the atom in that it is
an ion. A fifth theory is held by
idiots, but it is doubtful if they
know any more about the matter
than the others.

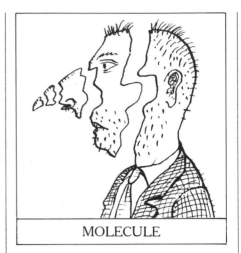

MOLECULE

MONAD, *n.*
The ultimate, indivisible unit of
matter. (See MOLECULE.) According
to Leibnitz, as nearly as he seems
willing to be understood, the monad
has body without bulk, and mind
without manifestation — Leibnitz
knows him by the innate power of
considering. He has founded upon
him a theory of the universe, which
the creature bears without
resentment, for the monad is a
gentleman. Small as he is, the
monad contains all the powers and
possibilities needful to his evolution
into a German philosopher of the
first class — altogether a very
capable little fellow. He is not to be
confounded with the microbe, or
bacillus; by its inability to discern
him, a good microscope shows him
to be of an entirely distinct species.

MONARCH, *n.*
A person engaged in reigning.
Formerly the monarch ruled, as the
derivation of the word attests, and
as many subjects have had occasion
to learn. In Russia and the Orient
the monarch has still a considerable
influence in public affairs and in
the disposition of the human head,
but in western Europe political
administration is mostly entrusted
to his ministers, he being somewhat
preoccupied with reflection relating
to the status of his own head.

MONARCHICAL GOVERNMENT, *n.*
Government.

MONDAY, *n.*
In Christian countries, the day after
the baseball game.

MONEY, *n.*
A blessing that is of no advantage
to us excepting when we part with
it. An evidence of culture and a
passport to polite society.
Supportable property.

MONKEY, *n.*
An arboreal animal which makes
itself at home in genealogical trees.

MONOSYLLABIC, *adj.*
Composed of words of one syllable,
for literary babes who never tire of
testifying their delight in the vapid
compound by appropriate
googoogling. The words are
commonly Saxon — that is to say,
words of a barbarous people
destitute of ideas and incapable of
any but the most elementary
sentiments and emotions.

> The man who writes in Saxon
> Is the man to use an ax on.
> *Judibras.*

MONSIGNOR, *n.*
A high ecclesiastical title, of which
the Founder of our religion
overlooked the advantages.

MONUMENT, *n.*
A structure intended to
commemorate something which
either needs no commemoration or
cannot be commemorated.

MORAL, *adj.*
Conforming to a local and mutable
standard of right. Having the
quality of general expediency.

MOUTH, *n.*
In man, the gateway to the soul; in
woman, the outlet of the heart.

MUGWUMP, *n.*
In politics one afflicted with self-
respect and addicted to the vice of
independence. A term of contempt.

MULATTO, *n.*
A child of two races, ashamed of
both.

MULTITUDE, *n.*
A crowd; the source of political
wisdom and virtue. In a republic,
the object of the statesman's
adoration. "In a multitude of
counsellors there is wisdom," saith
the proverb. If many men of equal
individual wisdom are wiser than
any one of them, it must be that
they acquire the excess of wisdom
by the mere act of getting together.
Whence comes it? Obviously from
nowhere — as well say that a range
of mountains is higher than the
single mountain composing it. A
multitude is as wise as its wisest
member if it obey him; if not, it is
no wiser than its most foolish.

MUMMY, *n.*
An ancient Egyptian, formerly in
universal use among modern
civilized nations as medicine, and
now engaged in supplying art with
an excellent pigment. He is handy,
too, in museums in gratifying the
vulgar curiosity that serves to
distinguish man from the lower
animals.

MYTHOLOGY, *n.*
The body of a primitive people's
beliefs concerning its origin, early
history, heroes, deities and so forth,
as distinguished from the true
accounts which it invents later.

N

NECTAR, *n.*

A drink served at banquets of the Olympian deities. The secret of its preparation is lost, but the modern Kentuckians believe that they come pretty near to a knowledge of its chief ingredient

> Juno drank a cup of nectar,
> But the draught did not affect her.
> Juno drank a cup of rye—
> Then she bade herself good-bye
>
> *J. G.*

NEGRO, *n.*

The *pièce de résistance* in the American political problem. Representing him by the letter *n*, the Republicans begin to build their equation thus: "Let *n* = the white man." This, however, appears to give an unsatisfactory solution.

NEIGHBOR, *n.*

One whom we are commanded to love as ourselves, and who does all he knows how to make us disobedient.

NEPOTISM, *n.*

Appointing your grandmother to office for the good of the party.

NEWTONIAN, *adj.*

Pertaining to a philosophy of the universe, invented by Newton, who discovered that an apple will fall to the ground, but was unable to say why. His successors and disciples have advanced so far as to be able to say when.

NIHILIST, *n.*

A Russian who denies the existence of anything but Tolstoi. The leader of the school is Tolstoi.

NIRVANA, *n.*

In the Buddhist religion, a state of pleasurable annihilation awarded to the wise, particularly to those wise enough to understand it.

NOBLEMAN, *n.*

Nature's provision for wealthy American maids ambitious to incur social distinction and suffer high life.

NOISE, *n.*

A stench in the ear. Undomesticated music. The chief product and authenticating sign of civilization.

NOMINATE, *v.*

To designate for the heaviest political assessment. To put forward a suitable person to incur the mudgobbing and deadcatting of the opposition.

NOMINEE, *n.*

A modest gentleman shrinking from the distinction of private life and diligently seeking the honorable obscurity of public office.

NON-COMBATANT, *n.*

A dead Quaker.

NONSENSE, *n.*

The objections that are urged against this excellent dictionary.

NOSE, *n.*

The extreme outpost of the face. From the circumstance that great conquerors have great noses, Getius, whose writings antedate the age of humor, calls the nose the organ of quell. It has been observed that one's nose is never so happy as when thrust into the affairs of another, from which some physiologists have drawn the inference that the nose is devoid of the sense of smell.

NOTORIETY, *n.*

The fame of one's competitor for public honors. The kind of renown most accessible and acceptable to mediocrity.

NOISE

O

OATH, *n.*
In law, a solemn appeal to the
Deity, made binding upon the
conscience by a penalty for perjury.

OBLIVION, *n.*
The state or condition in which the
wicked cease from struggling and
the dreary are at rest. Fame's
eternal dumping ground. Cold
storage for high hopes. A place
where ambitious authors meet their
works without pride and their
betters without envy. A dormitory
without an alarm clock.

OBSESSED, *pp.*
Vexed by an evil spirit, like the
Gadarene swine and other critics.
Obsession was once more common
than it is now. Arasthus tells of a
peasant who was occupied by a
different devil for every day in the
week, and on Sundays by two. They
were frequently seen, always
walking in his shadow, when he
had one, but were finally driven
away by the village notary, a holy
man; but they took the peasant with
them, for he vanished utterly. A
devil thrown out of a woman by the
Archbishop of Rheims ran through
the streets, pursued by a hundred
persons, until the open country was
reached, where by a leap higher
than a church spire he escaped into
a bird.

OBSESSED

OBSOLETE, *adj.*
No longer used by the timid. Said
chiefly of words. A word which
some lexicographer has marked
obsolete is ever thereafter an object
of dread and loathing to the fool
writer, but if it is a good word and
has no exact modern equivalent
equally good, it is good enough for
the good writer. Indeed, a writer's
attitude toward "obsolete" words is
as true a measure of his literary
ability as anything except the
character of his work. A dictionary
of obsolete and obsolescent words
would not only be singularly rich in
strong and sweet parts of speech; it
would add large possessions to the
vocabulary of every competent
writer who might not happen to be
a competent reader.

OBSTINATE, *adj.*
Inaccessible to the truth as it is
manifest in the splendor and stress
of our advocacy

The popular type and exponent of
obstinacy is the mule, a most
intelligent animal.

OCCASIONAL, *adj.*
Afflicting us with greater or less
frequency. That, however, is not the
sense in which the word is used in
the phrase "occasional verses,"
which are verses written for an
"occasion," such as an anniversary,
a celebration or other event. True,
they afflict us a little worse than
other sorts of verse, but their name
has no reference to irregular
recurrence.

OCCIDENT, *n.*
The part of the world lying west (or
east) of the Orient. It is largely
inhabited by Christians, a powerful
subtribe of the Hypocrites, whose
principal industries are murder
and cheating, which they are
pleased to call "war" and
"commerce." These, also, are the
principal industries of the Orient.

OCEAN

OCEAN, *n.*
A body of water occupying about two-thirds of a world made for man—who has no gills.

OFFENSIVE, *adj.*
Generating disagreeable emotions or sensations, as the advance of an army against its enemy.

"Were the enemy's tactics offensive?" the king asked. "I should say so!" replied the unsuccessful general. "The blackguard wouldn't come out of his works!"

OLD, *adj.*
In that stage of usefulness which is not inconsistent with general inefficiency, as an *old man.* Discredited by lapse of time and offensive to the popular taste, as an *old* book.

"Old books? The devil take them!"
Goby said.

"Fresh every day must be my books and bread."
Nature herself approves the Goby rule
And gives us every moment a fresh fool.

Harley Shum.

OLEAGINOUS, *adj.*
Oily, smooth, sleek.

Disraeli once described the manner of Bishop Wilberforce as "unctuous, oleaginous, saponaceous." And the good prelate was ever afterward known as Soapy Sam. For every man there is something in the vocabulary that would stick to him like a second skin. His enemies have only to find it.

OLYMPIAN, *adj.*
Relating to a mountain in Thessaly, once inhabited by gods, now a repository of yellowing newspapers, beer bottles and mutilated sardine cans, attesting the presence of the tourist and his appetite.

His name the smirking tourist
   scrawls
Upon Minerva's temple walls,
Where thundered once Olympian
   Zeus,
And marks his appetite's abuse.
             Averil Joop.

OMEN, *n.*
A sign that something will happen
if nothing happens.

ONCE, *adv.*
Enough.

OPERA, *n.*
A play representing life in another
world, whose inhabitants have no
speech but song, no motions but
gestures and no postures but
attitudes. All acting is simulation,
and the word *simulation* is from
simia, an ape; but in opera the
actor takes for his model *Simia
audibilis* (or *Pithecanthropos
stentor*)—the ape that howls.

   The actor apes a man—at least in
      shape;
   The opera performer apes an ape.

OPIATE, *n.*
An unlocked door in the prison of
Identity. It leads into the jail yard.

OPPORTUNITY, *n.*
A favorable occasion for grasping a
disappointment.

OPPOSE, *v.*
To assist with obstructions and
objections.

   How lonely he who thinks to vex
   With badinage the Solemn Sex!
   Of levity, Mere Man, beware;
   None but the Grave deserve the
      Unfair.
            Percy P. Orminder.

OPPOSITION, *n.*
In politics the party that prevents
the Government from running
amuck by hamstringing it.

The King of Ghargaroo, who had
been abroad to study the science of
government, appointed one hundred
of his fattest subjects as members
of a parliament to make laws for
the collection of revenue. Forty of
these he named the Party of
Opposition and had his Prime
Minister carefully instruct them in
their duty of opposing every royal
measure. Nevertheless, the first one
that was submitted passed
unanimously. Greatly displeased,
the King vetoed it, informing the
Opposition that if they did that
again they would pay for their
obstinacy with their heads. The
entire forty promptly disemboweled
themselves.

"What shall we do now?" the
King asked. "Liberal institutions
cannot be maintained without a
party of Opposition."

"Splendor of the universe," replied
the Prime Minister, "it is true these
dogs of darkness have no longer
their credentials, but all is not lost.
Leave the matter to this worm of
the dust."

So the Minister had the bodies of
his Majesty's Opposition embalmed
and stuffed with straw, put back
into the seats of power and nailed
there. Forty votes were recorded
against every bill and the nation
prospered. But one day a bill
imposing a tax on warts was
defeated—the members of the
Government party had not been
nailed to their seats! This so
enraged the King that the Prime
Minister was put to death, the
parliament was dissolved with a
battery of artillery, and
government of the people, by the
people, for the people perished from
Ghargaroo.

OPPOSITION

OPTIMISM, *n.*
The doctrine, or belief, that
everything is beautiful, including
what is ugly, everything good,
especially the bad, and everything
right that is wrong. It is held with
greatest tenacity by those most
accustomed to the mischance of
falling into adversity, and is most
acceptably expounded with the grin
that apes a smile. Being a blind
faith, it is inaccessible to the light
of disproof—an intellectual
disorder, yielding to no treatment
but death. It is hereditary, but
fortunately not contagious.

OPTIMIST, *n.*
A proponent of the doctrine that
black is white.

A pessimist applied to God for
relief.

"Ah, you wish me to restore your
hope and cheerfulness," said God.

"No," replied the petitioner, "I
wish you to create something that
would justify them."

"The world is all created," said
God, "but you have overlooked
something—the mortality of the
optimist."

ORATORY, *n.*
A conspiracy between speech and
action to cheat the understanding.
A tyranny tempered by
stenography.

ORPHAN, *n.*
A living person whom death has
deprived of the power of filial
ingratitude—a privation appealing
with a particular eloquence to all
that is sympathetic in human
nature. When young the orphan is
commonly sent to an asylum, where
by careful cultivation of its
rudimentary sense of locality it is
taught to know its place. It is then
instructed in the arts of dependence
and servitude and eventually
turned loose to prey upon the world
as a bootblack or scullery maid.

ORTHODOX, *n.*
An ox wearing the popular
religious yoke.

ORTHOGRAPHY, *n.*
The science of spelling by the eye
instead of the ear. Advocated with
more heat than light by the
outmates of every asylum for the
insane. They have had to concede a
few things since the time of
Chaucer, but are none the less hot
in defence of those to be conceded
hereafter.

> A spelling reformer indicted
> For fudge was before the court
>   cicted.
>   The judge said: "Enough—
>   His candle we'll snough,
> And his sepulchre shall not be
>   whicted."

OSTRICH, *n.*
A large bird to which (for its sins,
doubtless) nature has denied that
hinder toe in which so many pious
naturalists have seen a conspicuous
evidence of design. The absence of a
good working pair of wings is no
defect, for, as has been ingeniously
pointed out, the ostrich does not fly.

OTHERWISE, *adv.*
No better.

OUTCOME, *n.*
A particular type of disappointment. By the kind of intelligence
that sees in an exception a proof of
the rule the wisdom of an act is
judged by the outcome, the result.
This is immortal nonsense; the
wisdom of an act is to be judged by
the light that the doer had when he
performed it.

OUTDO, *v. t.*
To make an enemy.

OUT-OF-DOORS, *n.*
That part of one's environment
upon which no government has
been able to collect taxes.

OVATION, *n.*
In ancient Rome, a definite, formal
pageant in honor of one who had
been disserviceable to the enemies
of the nation. A lesser "triumph." In
modern English the word is
improperly used to signify any loose
and spontaneous expression of
popular homage to the hero of the
hour and place.

> "I had an ovation!" the actor man
>   said,
>   But I thought it uncommonly
>   queer,
> That people and critics by him had
>   been led
>   By the ear.
>
> The Latin lexicon makes his absurd
>   Assertion as plain as a peg;
> In "ovum" we find the true root of
>   the word.
>   It means egg.
> *Dudley Spink.*

OVEREAT, *v.*
To dine.

> Hail, Gastronome, Apostle of Excess,
> Well skilled to overeat without
>   distress!
> Thy great invention, the unfatal
>   feast,
> Shows Man's superiority to Beast.
> *John Boop.*

OVERWORK, *n.*
A dangerous disorder affecting
high public functionaries who want
to go fishing.

OWE, *v.*
To have (and to hold) a debt. The
word formerly signified not
indebtedness, but possession; it
meant "own," and in the minds of
debtors there is still a good deal of
confusion between assets and
liabilities.

OYSTER, *n.*
A slimy, gobby shellfish which
civilization gives men the hardihood
to eat without removing its entrails!
The shells are sometimes given to
the poor.

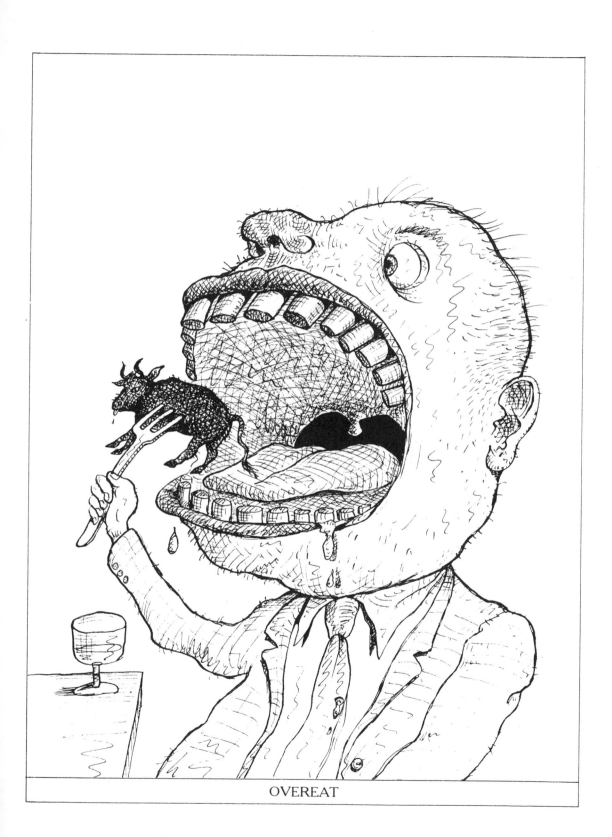

OVEREAT

P

PAIN, *n.*
An uncomfortable frame of mind that may have a physical basis in something that is being done to the body, or may be purely mental, caused by the good fortune of another.

PAINTING, *n.*
The art of protecting flat surfaces from the weather and exposing them to the critic.

Formerly, painting and sculpture were combined in the same work: the ancients painted their statues. The only present alliance between the two arts is that the modern painter chisels his patrons.

PALACE, *n.*
A fine and costly residence, particularly that of a great official. The residence of a high dignitary of the Christian Church is called a palace; that of the Founder of his religion was known as a field, or wayside. There is progress.

PALM, *n.*
A species of tree having several varieties, of which the familiar "itching palm" (*Palma hominis)* is most widely distributed and sedulously cultivated. This noble vegetable exudes a kind of invisible gum, which may be detected by applying to the bark a piece of gold or silver. The metal will adhere with remarkable tenacity. The fruit of the itching palm is so bitter and unsatisfying that a considerable percentage of it is sometimes given away in what are known as "benefactions."

PALMISTRY, *n.*
The 947th method (according to Mimbleshaw's classification) of obtaining money by false pretences. It consists in "reading character" in the wrinkles made by closing the hand. The pretence is not altogether false; character can really be read very accurately in this way, for the wrinkles in every hand submitted plainly spell the word "dupe." The imposture consists in not reading it aloud.

PANDEMONIUM, *n.*
Literally, the Place of All the Demons. Most of them have escaped into politics and finance, and the place is now used as a lecture hall by the Audible Reformer. When disturbed by his voice the ancient echoes clamor appropriate responses most gratifying to his pride of distinction.

PANTALOONS, *n.*
A nether habiliment of the adult civilized male. The garment is tubular and unprovided with hinges at the points of flexion. Supposed to have been invented by a humorist. Called "trousers" by the enlightened and "pants" by the unworthy.

PANTHEISM, *n.*
The doctrine that everything is God, in contradistinction to the doctrine that God is everything.

PANTOMIME, *n.*
A play in which the story is told without violence to the language. The least disagreeable form of dramatic action.

PARDON, *v.*
To remit a penalty and restore to a life of crime. To add to the lure of crime the temptation of ingratitude.

PASSPORT, *n.*
A document treacherously inflicted upon a citizen going abroad, exposing him as an alien and pointing him out for special reprobation and outrage.

PANTOMIME

PAST, *n.*
That part of Eternity with some small fraction of which we have a slight and regrettable acquaintance. A moving line called the Present parts it from an imaginary period known as the Future. These two grand divisions of Eternity, of which the one is continually effacing the other, are entirely unlike. The one is dark with sorrow and disappointment, the other bright with prosperity and joy. The Past is the region of sobs, the Future is the realm of song. In the one crouches Memory, clad in sackcloth and ashes, mumbling penitential prayer; in the sunshine of the other Hope flies with a free wing, beckoning to temples of success and bowers of ease. Yet the Past is the Future of yesterday, the Future is the Past of to-morrow. They are one—the knowledge and the dream.

PASTIME, *n.*
A device for promoting dejection. Gentle exercise for intellectual debility.

PATIENCE, *n.*
A minor form of despair, disguised as a virtue.

PATRIOT, *n.*
One to whom the interests of a part seem superior to those of the whole. The dupe of statesmen and the tool of conquerors.

PATRIOTISM, *n.*
Combustible rubbish ready to the torch of any one ambitious to illuminate his name.

    In Dr. Johnson's famous dictionary patriotism is defined as the last resort of a scoundrel. With all due respect to an enlightened but inferior lexicographer I beg to submit that it is the first.

PEACE, *n.*
In international affairs, a period of cheating between two periods of fighting.

> O, what's the loud uproar assailing
>   Mine ears without cease?
> 'Tis the voice of the hopeful, all-
>   hailing
>   The horrors of peace.
>
> Ah, Peace Universal; they woo it—
>   Would marry it, too.
> If only they knew how to do it
>   'Twere easy to do.
>
> They're working by night and by
>   day
>   On their problem, like moles.
> Have mercy, O Heaven, I pray,
>   On their meddlesome souls!
>   *Ro Amil.*

PEDESTRIAN, *n.*
The variable (and audible) part of the roadway for an automobile.

PEDIGREE, *n.*
The known part of the route from an arboreal ancestor with a swim bladder to an urban descendant with a cigarette.

PENITENT, *adj.*
Undergoing or awaiting punishment.

PERFECTION, *n.*
An imaginary state or quality distinguished from the actual by an element known as excellence; an attribute of the critic.

    The editor of an English magazine having received a letter pointing out the erroneous nature of his views and style, and signed "Perfection," promptly wrote at the foot of the letter: "I don't agree with you," and mailed it to Matthew Arnold.

PERIPATETIC, *adj.*
Walking about. Relating to the philosophy of Artistole, who, while expounding it, moved from place to

place in order to avoid his pupil's objections. A needless precaution — they knew no more of the matter than he.

PERORATION, *n.*
The explosion of an oratorical rocket. It dazzles, but to an observer having the wrong kind of nose its most conspicuous peculiarity is the smell of the serveral kinds of powder used in preparing it.

PERSEVERANCE, *n.*
A lowly virtue whereby mediocrity achieves an inglorious success.

> "Persevere, persevere!" cry the
> homilists all,
> Themselves, day and night,
> persevering to bawl.
> "Remember the fable of tortoise and
> hare —
> The one at the goal while the other
> is — where?"
> Why, back there in Dreamland,
> renewing his lease
> Of life, all his muscles preserving
> the peace,
> The goal and the rival forgotten
> alike,
> And the long fatigue of the needless
> hike.
> His spirit a-squat in the grass and
> the dew
> Of the dogless Land beyond the
> Stew,
> He sleeps, like a saint in a holy
> place,
> A winner of all that is good in a
> race.
> *Sukker Uffro.*

PESSIMISM, *n.*
A philosophy forced upon the convictions of the observer by the disheartening prevalence of the optimist with his scarecrow hope and his unsightly smile.

PHILANTHROPIST, *n.*
A rich (and usually bald) old gentleman who has trained himself to grin while his conscience is picking his pocket.

PHILISTINE, *n.*
One whose mind is the creature of its environment, following the fashion in thought, feeling and sentiment. He is sometimes learned, frequently prosperous, commonly clean and always solemn.

PHILOSOPHY, *n.*
A route of many roads leading from nowhere to nothing.

PHOENIX, *n.*
The classical prototype of the modern "small hot bird."

PHONOGRAPH, *n.*
An irritating toy that restores life to dead noises.

PHOTOGRAPH

PHOTOGRAPH, *n.*
A picture painted by the sun without instruction in art. It is a little better than the work of an Apache, but not quite so good as that of a Cheyenne.

PHRENOLOGY, *n.*
The science of picking the pocket through the scalp. It consists in locating and exploiting the organ that one is a dupe with.

PHYSICIAN, *n.*
One upon whom we set our hopes when ill and our dogs when well.

PHYSIOGNOMY, *n.*
The art of determining the
character of another by the
resemblances and differences
between his face and our own,
which is the standard of excellence.

PIANO, *n.*
A parlor utensil for subduing the
impenitent visitor. It is operated by
depressing the keys of the machine
and the spirits of the audience.

PICKANINNY, *n.*
The young of the *Procyanthropos*, or
Americanus dominans. It is small,
black and charged with political
fatalities.

PICTURE, *n.*
A representation in two dimensions
of something wearisome in three.

> "Behold great Daubert's picture
> here on view—
> Taken from Life." If that
> description's true,
> Grant, heavenly Powers, that I be
> taken, too.
> *Jali Hane.*

PIE, *n.*
An advance agent of the reaper
whose name is Indigestion.

> Cold pie was highly esteemed by the
> remains.—*The Rev. Dr. Mucker, in a
> Funeral Sermon Over a British
> Nobleman.*

PIETY, *n.*
Reverence for the Supreme Being,
based upon His supposed
resemblance to man.

> The pig is taught by sermons and
> epistles
> To think the God of Swine has snout
> and bristles.
> *Judibras.*

PIG

PIG, *n.*
An animal (*Porcus omnivorus*)
closely allied to the human race by
the splendor and vivacity of its
appetite, which, however, is inferior
in scope, for it sticks at pig.

PIGMY, *n.*
One of a tribe of very small men
found by ancient travelers in many
parts of the world, but by modern
in Central Africa only. The Pigmies
are so called to distinguish them
from the bulkier Caucasians—who
are Hogmies.

PILGRIM, *n.*
A traveler that is taken seriously. A
Pilgrim Father was one who,
leaving Europe in 1620 because not
permitted to sing psalms through
his nose, followed it to
Massachusetts, where he could
personate God according to the
dictates of his conscience.

PILLORY, *n.*
A mechanical device for inflicting
personal distinction—prototype of
the modern newspaper conducted
by persons of austere virtues and
blameless lives.

PIRACY, *n.*
Commerce without its folly-
swaddles, just as God made it.

PHYSIOGNOMY

PITIFUL, *adj.*
The state of an enemy or opponent
after an imaginary encounter with
oneself.

PITY, *n.*
A failing sense of exemption,
inspired by contrast.

PLAGIARISM, *n.*
A literary coincidence compounded
of a discreditable priority and an
honorable subsequence.

PLAGIARIZE, *v.*
To take the thought or style of
another writer whom one has never,
never read.

PLAGUE, *n.*
In ancient times a general
punishment of the innocent for
admonition of their ruler, as in the
familiar instance of Pharaoh the
Immune. The plague as we of to-
day have the happiness to know it is
merely Nature's fortuitous
manifestation of her purposeless
objectionableness.

PLAN, *v. t.*
To bother about the best method of
accomplishing an accidental result.

PLATITUDE, *n.*
The fundamental element and
special glory of popular literature.
A thought that snores in words that
smoke. The wisdom of a million
fools in the diction of a dullard. A
fossil sentiment in artificial rock. A
moral without the fable. All that is
mortal of a departed truth. A demi-
tasse of milk-and-morality. The
Pope's-nose of a featherless peacock.
A jelly-fish withering on the shore
of the sea of thought. The cackle
surviving the egg. A desiccated
epigram.

PLATONIC, *adj.*
Pertaining to the philosophy of
Socrates. Platonic Love is a fool's
name for the affection between a
disability and a frost.

PLAUDITS, *n.*
Coins with which the populace pays
those who tickle and devour it.

PLEASE, *v.*
To lay the foundation for a
superstructure of imposition.

PLEASURE, *n.*
The least hateful form of dejection.

PLEBEIAN, *n.*
An ancient Roman who in the blood
of his country stained nothing but
his hands. Distinguished from the
Patrician, who was a saturated
solution.

PLEBISCITE, *n.*
A popular vote to ascertain the will
of the sovereign.

PLENIPOTENTIARY, *adj.*
Having full power. A Minister
Plenipotentiary is a diplomatist
possessing absolute authority on
condition that he never exert it.

PLEONASM, *n.*
An army of words escorting a
corporal of thought.

PLOW, *n.*
An implement that cries aloud for
hands accustomed to the pen.

PLUNDER, *v.*
To take the property of another
without observing the decent and
customary reticences of theft. To
effect a change of ownership with
the candid concomitance of a brass
band. To wrest the wealth of A
from B and leave C lamenting a
vanished opportunity.

POCKET, *n.*
The cradle of motive and the grave of conscience. In woman this organ is lacking; so she acts without motive, and her conscience, denied burial, remains ever alive, confessing the sins of others.

POETRY, *n.*
A form of expression peculiar to the Land beyond the Magazines.

POKER, *n.*
A game said to be played with cards for some purpose to this lexicographer unknown.

POLICE, *n.*
An armed force for protection and participation.

POLITENESS, *n.*
The most acceptable hypocrisy.

POLITICIAN, *n.*
An eel in the fundamental mud upon which the superstructure of organized society is reared. When he wriggles he mistakes the agitation of his tail for the trembling of the edifice. As compared with the statesman, he suffers the disadvantage of being alive.

POLITICS, *n.*
A strife of interests masquerading as a contest of principles. The conduct of public affairs for private advantage.

POLYGAMY, *n.*
A house of atonement, or expiatory chapel, fitted with several stools of repentance, as distinguished from monogamy, which has but one.

POPULIST, *n.*
A fossil patriot of the early agricultural period, found in the old red soapstone underlying Kansas; characterized by an uncommon spread of ear, which some naturalists contend gave him the power of flight, though Professors Morse and Whitney, pursuing independent lines of thought, have ingeniously pointed out that had he possessed it he would have gone elsewhere. In the picturesque speech of his period, some fragments of which have come down to us, he was known as "The Matter with Kansas."

PORTABLE, *adj.*
Exposed to a mutable ownership through vicissitudes of possession.

> His light estate, if neither he did
>   make it
> Nor yet its former guardian forsake
>   it,
> Is portable improperty, I take it.
> *Worgum Slupsky.*

PORTUGUESE, *n. pl.*
A species of geese indigenous to Portugal. They are mostly without feathers and imperfectly edible, even when stuffed with garlic.

POSITIVE, *adj.*
Mistaken at the top of one's voice.

POSITIVISM, *n.*
A philosophy that denies our knowledge of the Real and affirms our ignorance of the Apparent. Its longest exponent is Comte, its broadest Mill and its thickest Spencer.

POSTERITY, *n.*
An appellate court which reverses the judgment of a popular author's contemporaries, the appellant being his obscure competitor.

POTABLE, *n.*
Suitable for drinking. Water is said
to be potable; indeed, some declare
it our natural beverage, although
even they find it palatable only
when suffering from the recurrent
disorder known as thirst, for which
it is a medicine. Upon nothing has
so great and diligent ingenuity been
brought to bear in all ages and in
all countries, except the most
uncivilized, as upon the invention of
substitutes for water. To hold that
this general aversion to that liquid
has no basis in the preservative
instinct of the race is to be
unscientific — and without science
we are as the snakes and toads.

POVERTY, *n.*
A file provided for the teeth of the
rats of reform. The number of plans
for its abolition equals that of the
reformers who suffer from it, plus
that of the philosophers who know
nothing about it. Its victims are
distinguished by possession of all
the virtues and by their faith in
leaders seeking to conduct them
into a prosperity where they believe
these to be unknown.

PRAY, *v.*
To ask that the laws of the universe
be annulled in behalf of a single
petitioner confessedly unworthy.

PRE-ADAMITE, *n.*
One of an experimental and
apparently unsatisfactory race that
antedated Creation and lived under
conditions not easily conceived.
Melsius believed them to have
inhabited "the Void" and to have
been something intermediate
between fishes and birds. Little is
known of them beyond the fact that
they supplied Cain with a wife and
theologians with a controversy.

PRECEDENT, *n.*
In Law, a previous decision, rule or
practice which, in the absence of a
definite statute, has whatever force
and authority a Judge may choose
to give it, thereby greatly
simplifying his task of doing as he
pleases. As there are precedents for
everything, he has only to ignore
those that make against his interest
and accentuate those in the line of
his desire. Invention of the
precedent elevates the trial-at-law
from the low estate of a fortuitous
ordeal to the noble attitude of a
dirigible arbitrament.

PRECIPITATE, *adj.*
Anteprandial.

> Precipitate in all, this sinner
> Took action first, and then his
> dinner.
> *Judibras.*

PREDESTINATION, *n.*
The doctrine that all things occur
according to programme. This
doctrine should not be confused
with that of foreordination, which
means that all things are
programmed, but does not affirm
their occurrence, that being only an
implication from other doctrines by
which this is entailed. The
difference is great enough to have
deluged Christendom with ink, to
say nothing of the gore. With the
distinction of the two doctrines kept
well in mind, and a reverent belief
in both, one may hope to escape
perdition if spared.

PREDICAMENT, *n.*
The wage of consistency.

PREDILECTION, *n.*
The preparatory stage of
disillusion.

PRE-EXISTENCE, *n.*
An unnoted factor in creation.

PRE-EXISTENCE

PREFERENCE, *n.*
A sentiment, or frame of mind, induced by the erroneous belief that one thing is better than another.

An ancient philosopher, expounding his conviction that life is no better than death, was asked by a disciple why, then, he did not die. "Because," he replied, "death is no better than life."

It is longer.

PREHISTORIC, *adj.*
Belonging to an early period and a museum. Antedating the art and practice of perpetuating falsehood.

> He lived in a period prehistoric,
> When all was absurd and
>   phantasmagoric.
> Born later, when Clio, celestial
>   recorder,
> Set down great events in succession
>   and order,
> He surely had seen nothing droll or
>   fortuitous
> In anything here but the lies that
>   she threw at us.
> *Orpheus Bowen.*

PREJUDICE, *n.*
A vagrant opinion without visible means of support.

PRELATE, *n.*
A church officer having a superior degree of holiness and a fat preferment. One of Heaven's aristocracy. A gentleman of God.

PREROGATIVE, *n.*
A sovereign's right to do wrong.

PRESBYTERIAN, *n.*
One who holds the conviction that the governing authorities of the Church should be called presbyters.

PRESCRIPTION, *n.*
A physician's guess at what will best prolong the situation with least harm to the patient.

PRESIDE

PRESENT, *n.*
That part of eternity dividing the
domain of disappointment from the
realm of hope.

PRESENTABLE, *adj.*
Hideously appareled after the
manner of the time and place.

In Boorioboola-Gha a man is
presentable on occasions of
ceremony if he have his abdomen
painted a bright blue and wear a
cow's tail; in New York he may, if
it please him, omit the paint, but
after sunset he must wear two tails
made of the wool of a sheep and
dyed black.

PRESIDE, *v.*
To guide the action of a deliberative
body to a desirable result. In
Journalese, to perform upon a
musical instrument; as, "He
presided at the piccolo."

> The Headliner, holding the copy in
>   hand,
>   Read with a solemn face:
> "The music was very uncommonly
>   grand —
>   The best that was ever provided,
>   For our townsman Brown
>   presided
>   At the organ with skill and
>   grace."
> The Headliner discontinued to read,
>   And, spreading the paper down
> On the desk, he dashed in at the top
>   of the screed:
> "Great playing by President
>   Brown."
>
> *Orpheus Bowen.*

PRESIDENCY, *n.*
The greased pig in the field game
of American politics.

PRESIDENT, *n.*
The leading figure in a small group
of men of whom — and of whom
only — it is positively known that
immense numbers of their
countrymen did not want any of
them for President.

> If that's an honor surely 'tis a
>   greater
> To have been a simple and
>   undamned spectator.
> Behold in me a man of mark and
>   note
> Whom no elector e'er denied a
>   vote! —
> An undiscredited, unhooted gent
> Who might, for all we know, be
>   President
> By acclamation. Cheer, ye varlets,
>   cheer —
> I'm passing with a wide and open
>   ear!
>
> *Jonathan Fomry.*

PREVARICATOR, *n.*
A liar in the caterpillar state.

PRICE, *n.*
Value, plus a reasonable sum for
the wear and tear of conscience in
demanding it.

PRIMATE, *n.*
The head of a church, especially a
State church supported by
involuntary contributions. The
Primate of England is the
Archbishop of Canterbury, an
amiable old gentleman, who
occupies Lambeth Palace when
living and Westminster Abbey
when dead. He is commonly dead.

PRISON, *n.*
A place of punishments and
rewards. The poet assures us that —

> "Stone walls do not a prison make,"

but a combination of the stone wall,
the political parasite and the moral
instructor is no garden of sweets.

PRIVATE, *n.*
A military gentleman with a field-
marshal's baton in his knapsack
and an impediment in his hope.

PROBOSCIS, *n.*
The rudimentary organ of an
elephant which serves him in place
of the knife-and-fork that Evolution
has as yet denied him. For purposes
of humor it is popularly called a
trunk.

Asked how he knew that an
elephant was going on a journey,
the illustrious Jo. Miller cast a
reproachful look upon his
tormentor, and answered, absently:
"When it is ajar," and threw
himself from a high promontory
into the sea. Thus perished in his
pride the most famous humorist of
antiquity, leaving to mankind a
heritage of woe! No successor
worthy of the title has appeared,
though Mr. Edward Bok, of *The
Ladies' Home Journal,* is much
respected for the purity and
sweetness of his personal character.

PROJECTILE, *n.*
The final arbiter in international
disputes. Formerly these disputes
were settled by physical contact of
the disputants, with such simple
arguments as the rudimentary logic
of the times could supply—the
sword, the spear, and so forth. With
the growth of prudence in military
affairs the projectile came more
and more into favor, and is now
held in high esteem by the most
courageous. Its capital defect is that
it requires personal attendance at
the point of propulsion.

PROOF, *n.*
Evidence having a shade more of
plausibility than of unlikelihood.
The testimony of two credible
witnesses as opposed to that of only
one.

PROOF-READER, *n.*
A malefactor who atones for
making your writing nonsense by
permitting the compositor to make
it unintelligible.

PROPERTY, *n.*
Any material thing, having no
particular value, that may be held
by A against the cupidity of B.
Whatever gratifies the passion for
possession in one and disappoints it
in all others. The object of man's
brief rapacity and long
indifference.

PROPHECY, *n.*
The art and practice of selling one's
credibility for future delivery.

PROSPECT, *n.*
An outlook, usually forbidding. An
expectation, usually forbidden.

> Blow, blow, ye spicy breezes—
> O'er Ceylon blow your breath,
> Where every prospect pleases,
> Save only that of death.
> *Bishop Sheber.*

PROVIDENTIAL, *adj.*
Unexpectedly and conspicuously
beneficial to the person so
describing it.

PRUDE, *n.*
A bawd hiding behind the back of
her demeanor.

PUBLISH, *v.*
In literary affairs, to become the
fundamental element in a cone of
critics.

PUSH, *n.*
One of the two things mainly
conducive to success, especially in
politics. The other is Pull.

PYRRHONISM, *n.*
An ancient philosophy, named for
its inventor. It consisted of an
absolute disbelief in everything but
Pyrrhonism. Its modern professors
have added that.

Q

QUEEN, *n.*
A woman by whom the realm is ruled when there is a king, and through whom it is ruled when there is not.

QUILL, *n.*
An implement of torture yielded by a goose and commonly wielded by an ass. This use of the quill is now obsolete, but its modern equivalent, the steel pen, is wielded by the same everlasting Presence.

QUIVER, *n.*
A portable sheath in which the ancient statesman and the aboriginal lawyer carried their lighter arguments.

> He extracted from his quiver,
> Did this controversial Roman,
> An argument well fitted
> To the question as submitted,
> Then addressed it to the liver,
> Of the unpersuaded foeman.
> *Oglum P. Boomp.*

QUIXOTIC, *adj.*
Absurdly chivalric, like Don Quixote. An insight into the beauty and excellence of this incomparable adjective is unhappily denied to him who has the misfortune to know that the gentleman's name is pronounced Ke-ho-tay.

> When ignorance from out our lives
>   can banish
> Philology, 'tis folly to know Spanish.
> *Juan Smith.*

QUORUM, *n.*
A sufficient number of members of a deliberative body to have their own way and their own way of having it. In the United States Senate a quorum consists of the chairman of the Committee on Finance and a messenger from the White House; in the House of Representatives, of the Speaker and the devil.

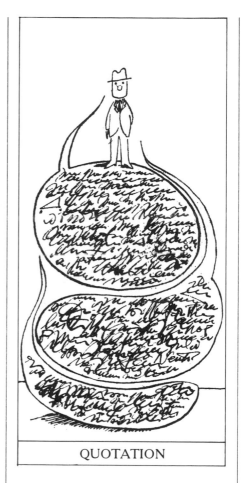

QUOTATION

QUOTATION, *n.*
The act of repeating erroneously the words of another. The words erroneously repeated.

> Intent on making his quotation
>   truer,
> He sought the page infallible of
>   Brewer,
> Then made a solemn vow that he
>   would be
> Condemned eternally. Ah, me, ah,
>   me!
> *Stumpo Gaker.*

QUOTIENT, *n.*
A number showing how many times a sum of money belonging to one person is contained in the pocket of another—usually about as many times as it can be got there.

R

RABBLE, *n.*
In a republic, those who exercise a supreme authority tempered by fraudulent elections. The rabble is like the sacred Simurgh, of Arabian fable—omnipotent on condition that it do nothing. (The word is Aristocratese, and has no exact equivalent in our tongue, but means, as nearly as may be, "soaring swine.")

RACK, *n.*
An argumentative implement formerly much used in persuading devotees of a false faith to embrace the living truth. As a call to the unconverted the rack never had any particular efficacy, and is now held in light popular esteem.

RADICALISM, *n.*
The conservatism of to-morrow injected into the affairs of to-day.

RADIUM, *n.*
A mineral that gives off heat and stimulates the organ that a scientist is a fool with.

RAILROAD, *n.*
The chief of many mechanical devices enabling us to get away from where we are to where we are no better off. For this purpose the railroad is held in highest favor by the optimist, for it permits him to make the transit with great expedition.

RACK

RAMSHACKLE

RAMSHACKLE, *adj.*
Pertaining to a certain order of architecture, otherwise known as the Normal American. Most of the public buildings of the United States are of the Ramshackle order, though some of our earlier architects preferred the Ironic. Recent additions to the White House in Washington are Theo-Doric, the ecclesiastic order of the Dorians. They are exceedingly fine and cost one hundred dollars a brick.

RANK, *n.*
Relative elevation in the scale of human worth.

> He held at court a rank so high
> That other noblemen asked why.
> "Because," 'twas answered, "others lack
> His skill to scratch the royal back."
> *Aramis Jukes.*

RANSOM, *n.*
The purchase of that which neither belongs to the seller, nor can belong to the buyer. The most unprofitable of investments.

RAPACITY, *n.*
Providence without industry. The thrift of power.

RAREBIT, *n.*
A Welsh rabbit, in the speech of the humorless, who point out that it is not a rabbit. To whom it may be solemnly explained that the comestible known as toad-in-a-hole is really not a toad, and that *riz-de-veau à la financière* is not the smile of a calf prepared after the recipe of a she banker.

RASCAL, *n.*
A fool considered under another aspect.

RASCALITY, *n.*
Stupidity militant. The activity of a clouded intellect.

RASH, *adj.*
Insensible to the value of our advice.

> "Now lay your bet with mine, nor let
> These gamblers take your cash."
> "Nay, this child makes no bet."
> "Great snakes!
> How can you be so rash?"
> *Bootle P. Gish.*

RATIONAL, *adj.*
Devoid of all delusions save those of observation, experience and reflection.

RATTLESNAKE, *n.*
Our prostrate brother, *Homo ventrambulans.*

RAZOR, *n.*
An instrument used by the
Caucasian to enhance his beauty, by
the Mongolian to make a guy of
himself, and by the Afro-American
to affirm his worth.

REACH, *n.*
The radius of action of the human
hand. The area within which it is
possible (and customary) to gratify
directly the propensity to provide.

> This is a truth, as old as the hills,
>   That life and experience teach:
> The poor man suffers that keenest of
>   ills,
>   An impediment in his reach.
>   *G. J.*

READING, *n.*
The general body of what one
reads. In our country it consists, as
a rule, of Indiana novels, short
stories in "dialect" and humor in
slang.

> We know by one's reading
> His learning and breeding;
> By what draws his laughter
> We know his Hereafter.
> Read nothing, laugh never—
> The Sphinx was less clever!
>   *Jupiter Muke.*

READING

REALISM, *n.*
The art of depicting nature as it is
seen by toads. The charm suffusing
a landscape painted by a mole, or a
story written by a measuring-
worm.

REALITY, *n.*
The dream of a mad philosopher.
That which would remain in the
cupel if one should assay a
phantom. The nucleus of a vacuum.

REALLY, *adv.*
Apparently.

REAR, *n.*
In American military matters, that
exposed part of the army that is
nearest to Congress.

REASON, *v. i.*
To weigh probabilities in the scales
of desire.

REASON, *n.*
Propensitate of prejudice.

REASONABLE, *adj.*
Accessible to the infection of our
own opinions. Hospitable to
persuasion, dissuasion and evasion.

REBEL, *n.*
A proponent of a new misrule who
has failed to establish it.

RECOLLECT, *v.*
To recall with additions something
not previously known.

RECONCILIATION, *n.*
A suspension of hostilities. An
armed truce for the purpose of
digging up the dead.

RECONSIDER, *v.*
To seek a justification for a decision
already made.

REBEL

RECOUNT, *n.*
In American politics, another throw of the dice, accorded to the player against whom they are loaded.

RECREATION, *n.*
A particular kind of dejection to relieve a general fatigue.

RECRUIT, *n.*
A person distinguishable from a civilian by his uniform and from a soldier by his gait.

> Fresh from the farm or factory or
>   street,
> His marching, in pursuit or in
>   retreat,
>   Were an impressive martial
>   spectacle
> Except for two impediments — his
>   feet.
>   *Thompson Johnson.*

RECTOR, *n.*
In the Church of England, the Third Person of the parochial Trinity, the Curate and the Vicar being the other two.

REDEMPTION, *n.*
Deliverance of sinners from the penalty of their sin, through their murder of the deity against whom they sinned. The doctrine of Redemption is the fundamental mystery of our holy religion, and whoso believeth in it shall not perish, but have everlasting life in which to try to understand it.

> We must awake Man's spirit from
>   its sin,
>   And take some special measure
>   for redeeming it;
> Though hard indeed the task to get
>   it in
>   Among the angels any way but
>   teaming it,
>   Or purify it otherwise than
>   steaming it.
> I'm awkward at Redemption — a
>   beginner:
> My method is to crucify the sinner.
>   *Golgo Brone.*

REDRESS, *n.*
Reparation without satisfaction.

Among the Anglo-Saxons a subject conceiving himself wronged by the king was permitted, on proving his injury, to beat a brazen image of the royal offender with a switch that was afterward applied to his own naked back. The latter rite was performed by the public hangman, and it assured moderation in the plaintiff's choice of a switch.

RED-SKIN, *n.*
A North American Indian, whose skin is not red — at least not on the outside.

REDUNDANT, *adj.*
Superfluous; needless; *de trop.*

> The Sultan said: "There's evidence
>   abundant
> To prove this unbelieving dog
>   redundant."
> To whom the Grand Vizier, with
>   mien impressive,
> Replied: "His head, at least, appears
>   excessive."
>   *Habeeb Suleiman.*

> Mr. Debs is a redundant citizen.
>   — *Theodore Roosevelt.*

REFERENDUM, *n.*
A law for submission of proposed legislation to a popular vote to learn the nonsensus of public opinion.

REFLECTION, *n.*
An action of the mind whereby we obtain a clearer view of our relation to the things of yesterday and are able to avoid the perils that we shall not again encounter.

REFORM, *n.*
A thing that mostly satisfies reformers opposed to reformation.

REFLECTION

REFUGE, *n.*
Anything assuring protection to one in peril. Moses and Joshua provided six cities of refuge—Bezer, Golan, Ramoth, Kadesh, Schekem and Hebron—to which one who had taken life inadvertently could flee when hunted by relatives of the deceased. This admirable expedient supplied him with wholesome exercise and enabled them to enjoy the pleasures of the chase; whereby the soul of the dead man was appropriately honored by observances akin to the funeral games of early Greece.

REFUSAL, *n.*
Denial of something desired; as an elderly maiden's hand in marriage, to a rich and handsome suitor; a valuable franchise to a rich corporation, by an alderman; absolution to an impenitent king, by a priest, and so forth. Refusals are graded in a descending scale of finality thus: the refusal absolute, the refusal conditional, the refusal tentative and the refusal feminine. The last is called by some casuists the refusal assentive.

REGALIA, *n.*
Distinguishing insignia, jewels and costume of such ancient and honorable orders as Knights of Adam; Visionaries of Delectable Bosh; the Ancient Order of Modern Troglodytes; the League of Holy Humbug; the Golden Phalanx of Phalangers; the Genteel Society of Expurgated Hoodlums; the Mystic Alliance of Gorgeous Regalians; Knights and Ladies of the Yellow Dog; the Oriental Order of Sons of the West; the Blatherhood of Insufferable Stuff; Warriors of the Long Bow; Guardians of the Great Horn Spoon; the Band of Brutes; the Impenitent Order of Wife-Beaters; the Sublime Legion of Flamboyant Conspicuants; Worshipers at the Electroplated Shrine; Shining Inaccessibles; Fee-Faw-Fummers of the Inimitable Grip; Jannissaries of the Broad-Blown Peacock; Plumed Increscencies of the Magic Temple; the Grand Cabal of Able-Bodied Sedentarians; Associated Deities of the Butter Trade; the Garden of Galoots; the Affectionate Fraternity of Men Similarly Warted; the Flashing Astonishers; Ladies of Horror; Cooperative Association for Breaking into the Spotlight; Dukes of Eden; Disciples Militant of the Hidden Faith; Knights-Champions of the Domestic Dog; the Holy Gregarians; the Resolute Optimists; the Ancient Sodality of Inhospitable Hogs; Associated Sovereigns of Mendacity; Dukes-Guardian of the Mystic Cess-Pool; the Society for Prevention of Prevalence; Kings of Drink; Polite Federation of Gents-Consequential; the Mysterious Order of the Undecipherable Scroll; Uniformed Rank of Lousy Cats; Monarchs of Worth and Hunger; Sons of the South Star; Prelates of the Tub-and-Sword.

RELIGION, *n.*
A daughter of Hope and Fear, explaining to Ignorance the nature of the Unknowable.

"What is your religion my son?" inquired the Archbishop of Rheims.

"Pardon, monseigneur," replied Rochebriant; "I am ashamed of it."

"Then why do you not become an atheist?"

"Impossible! I should be ashamed of atheism."

"In that case, monseiur, you should join the Protestants."

RELIQUARY, *n.*
A receptacle for such sacred objects as pieces of the true cross, short-ribs of saints, the ears of Balaam's ass, the lung of the cock that called Peter to repentance and so forth. Reliquaries are commonly of metal, and provided with a lock to prevent the contents from coming out and performing miracles at unseasonable times. A feather from

the wing of the Angel of the Annunciation once escaped during a sermon in Saint Peter's and so tickled the noses of the congregation that they woke and sneezed with great vehemence three times each. It is related in the "Gesta Sanctorum" that a sacristan in the Canterbury cathedral surprised the head of Saint Dennis in the library. Reprimanded by its stern custodian, it explained that it was seeking a body of doctrine. This unseemly levity so enraged the diocesan that the offender was publicly anathematized, thrown into the Stour and replaced by another head of Saint Dennis, brought from Rome.

RENOWN, *n.*
A degree of distinction between notoriety and fame—a little more supportable than the one and a little more intolerable than the other. Sometimes it is conferred by an unfriendly and inconsiderate hand.

> I touched the harp in every key,
>   But found no heeding ear;
> And then Ithuriel touched me
>   With a revealing spear.
>
> Not all my genius, great as 'tis,
>   Could urge me out of night.
> I felt the faint appulse of his,
>   And leapt into the light!
>   *W. J. Candleton.*

REPARATION, *n.*
Satisfaction that is made for a wrong and deducted from the satisfaction felt in committing it.

REPARTEE, *n.*
Prudent insult in retort. Practiced by gentlemen with a constitutional aversion to violence, but a strong disposition to offend. In a war of words, the tactics of the North American Indian.

REPLICA, *n.*
A reproduction of a work of art, by

REPLICA

the artist that made the original. It is so called to distinguish it from a "copy," which is made by another artist. When the two are made with equal skill the replica is the more valuable, for it is supposed to be more beautiful than it looks.

REPORTER, *n.*
A writer who guesses his way to the truth and dispels it with a tempest of words.

> "More dear than all my bosom
>   knows, O thou
> Whose 'lips are sealed' and will not
>   disavow!"
> So sang the blithe reporter-man as
>   grew
> Beneath his hand the leg-long
>   "interview."
>   *Barson Maith.*

REPOSE, *v. i.*
To cease from troubling.

REPRESENTATIVE, *n.*
In national politics, a member of the Lower House in this world, and without discernible hope of promotion in the next.

REPROBATION, *n.*
In theology, the state of a luckless mortal prenatally damned. The doctrine of reprobation was taught by Calvin, whose joy in it was somewhat marred by the sad sincerity of his conviction that although some are foredoomed to perdition, others are predestined to salvation.

REPUBLIC, *n.*
A nation in which, the thing governing and the thing governed being the same, there is only a permitted authority to enforce an optional obedience. In a republic the foundation of public order is the ever lessening habit of submission inherited from ancestors who, being truly governed, submitted because they had to. There are as many kinds of republics as there are gradations between the despotism whence they came and the anarchy whither they lead.

REQUIEM, *n.*
A mass for the dead which the minor poets assure us the winds sing o'er the graves of their favorites. Sometimes, by way of providing a varied entertainment, they sing a dirge.

RESIDENT, *adj.*
Unable to leave.

RESIGN, *v. t.*
To renounce an honor for an advantage. To renounce an advantage for a greater advantage.

> 'Twas rumored Leonard Wood had
>   signed
>   A true renunciation
> Of title, rank and every kind
>   Of military station—
>   Each honorable station.
>
> By his example fired—inclined
>   To noble emulation,
> The country humbly was resigned
>   To Leonard's resignation—
>   His Christian resignation.
>   *Politian Greame.*

RESOLUTE, *adj.*
Obstinate in a course that we approve.

RESPECTABILITY, *n.*
The offspring of a *liaison* between a bald head and a bank account.

RESPIRATOR, *n.*
An apparatus fitted over the nose and mouth of an inhabitant of London, whereby to filter the visible universe in its passage to the lungs.

RESPITE, *n.*
A suspension of hostilities against a sentenced assassin, to enable the Executive to determine whether the murder may not have been done by the prosecuting attorney. Any break in the continuity of a disagreeable expectation.

RESPITE

RESPLENDENT, *adj.*
Like a simple American citizen
beduking himself in his lodge, or
affirming his consequence in the
Scheme of Things as an elemental
unit of a parade.

> The Knights of Dominion were so
> resplendent in their velvet-and-gold that
> their masters would hardly have known
> them. — *"Chronicles of the Classes."*

RESPOND, *v. i.*
To make answer, or disclose
otherwise a consciousness of having
inspired an interest in what
Herbert Spencer calls "external
coexistences," as Satan "squat like a
toad" at the ear of Eve, responded
to the touch of the angel's spear. To
respond in damages is to contribute
to the maintenance of the plaintiff's
attorney and, incidentally, to the
gratification of the plaintiff.

RESPONSIBILITY, *n.*
A detachable burden easily shifted
to the shoulders of God, Fate,
Fortune, Luck or one's neighbor. In
the days of astrology it was
customary to unload it upon a star.

> Alas, things ain't what we should see
> If Eve had let that apple be;
> And many a feller which had ought
> To set with monarchses of thought,
> Or play some rosy little game
> With battle-chaps on fields of fame,
> Is downed by his unlucky star,
> And hollers: "Peanuts! — here you
>   are!"
> > *"The Sturdy Beggar."*

RESTITUTION, *n.*
The founding or endowing of
universities and public libraries by
gift or bequest.

RESTITUTOR, *n.*
Benefactor; philanthropist.

RETALIATION, *n.*
The natural rock upon which is
reared the Temple of Law.

RETRIBUTION, *n.*
A rain of fire-and-brimstone that
falls alike upon the just and such of
the unjust as have not procured
shelter by evicting them.

In the lines following, addressed
to an Emperor in Exile by Father
Gassalasca Jape, the reverend poet
appears to hint his sense of the
imprudence of turning about to face
Retribution when it is taking
exercise:

> What, what! Dom Pedro, you desire
>   to go
>   Back to Brazil to end your days in
>   quiet?
> Why, what assurance have you
>   'twould be so?
>   'Tis not so long since you were in a
>   riot,
>   And your dear subjects showed a
>   will to fly at
> Your throat and shake you like a
>   rat. You know
> That empires are ungrateful; are
>   you certain
> Republics are less handy to get hurt
>   in?

REVEILLE

REVEILLE, *n.*
A signal to sleeping soldiers to
dream of battlefields no more, but
get up and have their blue noses
counted. In the American army it is
ingeniously called "rev-e-lee," and
to that pronunciation our
countrymen have pledged their
lives, their misfortunes and their
sacred dishonor.

REVELATION, *n.*
A famous book in which St. John
the Divine concealed all that he
knew. The revealing is done by the
commentators, who know nothing.

REVERENCE, *n.*
The spiritual attitude of a man to a
god and a dog to a man.

REVIEW, *v. t.*

> To set your wisdom (holding not a
>   doubt of it,
>   Although in truth there's neither
>   bone nor skin to it)
> At work upon a book, and so read
>   out of it
>   The qualities that you have first
>   read into it.

REVOLUTION, *n.*
In politics, an abrupt change in the
form of misgovernment.
Specifically, in American history,
the substitution of the rule of an
Administration for that of a
Ministry, whereby the welfare and
happiness of the people were
advanced a full half-inch.
Revolutions are usually
accompanied by a considerable
effusion of blood, but are accounted
worth it — this appraisement being
made by beneficiaries whose blood
had not the mischance to be shed.
The French revolution is of
incalculable value to the Socialist of
to-day; when he pulls the string
actuating its bones its gestures are
inexpressibly terrifying to gory
tyrants suspected of fomenting law
and order.

RHADOMANCER, *n.*
One who uses a divining-rod in
prospecting for precious metals in
the pocket of a fool.

RIBALDRY, *n.*
Censorious language by another
concerning oneself.

RIBROASTER, *n.*
Censorious language by oneself
concerning another. The word is of
classical refinement, and is even
said to have been used in a fable by
Georgius Coadjutor, one of the most
fastidious writers of the fifteenth
century — commonly, indeed,
regarded as the founder of the
Fastidiotic School.

RICE-WATER, *n.*
A mystic beverage secretly used by
our most popular novelists and
poets to regulate the imagination
and narcotize the conscience. It is
said to be rich in both obtundite
and lethargine, and is brewed in a
midnight fog by a fat witch of the
Dismal Swamp.

RICH, *adj.*
Holding in trust and subject to an
accounting the property of the
indolent, the incompetent, the
unthrifty, the envious and the
luckless. That is the view that
prevails in the underworld, where
the Brotherhood of Man finds its
most logical development and
candid advocacy. To denizens of the
midworld the word means good and
wise.

RICHES, *n.*

> A gift from Heaven signifying, "This
> is my beloved son, in whom I am well
> pleased." — *John D. Rockefeller.*

> The reward of toil and virtue. — *J. P.
> Morgan.*

> The savings of many in the hands of
> one. — *Eugene Debs.*

> To these excellent definitions the
> inspired lexicographer feels that he
> can add nothing of value.

RIDICULE, *n.*
Words designed to show that the
person of whom they are uttered is
devoid of the dignity of character
distinguishing him who utters
them. It may be graphic, mimetic
or merely rident. Shaftesbury is
quoted as having pronounced it the
test of truth — a ridiculous
assertion, for many a solemn fallacy
has undergone centuries of ridicule
with no abatement of its popular
acceptance. What, for example, has
been more valorously derided than
the doctrine of Infant
Respectability?

RIGHT, *n.*
Legitimate authority to be, to do or
to have; as the right to be a king,
the right to do one's neighbor, the
right to have measles, and the like.
The first of these rights was once
universally believed to be derived
directly from the will of God; and
this is still sometimes affirmed *in
partibus infidelium* outside the
enlightened realms of Democracy;
as the well known lines of Sir
Abednego Bink, following:

By what right, then, do royal rulers
    rule?
  Whose is the sanction of their state
    and pow'r?
He surely were as stubborn as a
    mule
  Who, God unwilling, could
      maintain an hour
His uninvited session on the throne, or
    air
His pride securely in the Presidential
    chair.

  Whatever is is so by Right Divine;
  Whate'er occurs, God wills it so.
    Good land!
  It were a wondrous thing if His
    design
    A fool could baffle or a rogue
      withstand!
If so, then God, I say (intending no
    offence)
Is guilty of contributory negligence.

RIGHTEOUSNESS, *n.*
A sturdy virtue that was once found
among the Pantidoodles inhabiting
the lower part of the peninsula of
Oque. Some feeble attempts were
made by returned missionaries to
introduce it into several European
countries, but it appears to have
been imperfectly expounded. An
example of this faulty exposition is
found in the only extant sermon of
the pious Bishop Rowley, a
characteristic passage from which
is here given:

"Now righteousness consisteth not
merely in a holy state of mind, nor yet in
performance of religious rites and
obedience to the letter of the law. It is not
enough that one be pious and just: one
must see to it that others also are in the
same state; and to this end compulsion is
a proper means. Forasmuch as my
injustice may work ill to another, so by
his injustice may evil be wrought upon
still another, the which it is as
manifestly my duty to estop as to
forestall mine own tort. Wherefore if I
would be righteous I am bound to
restrain my neighbor, by force if
needful, in all those injurious
enterprises from which, through a
better disposition and by the help of
Heaven, I do myself refrain."

RIME, *n.*
Agreeing sounds in the terminals of
verse, mostly bad. The verses
themselves, as distinguished from
prose, mostly dull. Usually (and
wickedly) spelled "rhyme."

RIMER, *n.*
A poet regarded with indifference
or disesteem.

The rimer quenches his unheeded
    fires,
The sound surceases and the sense
    expires.
Then the domestic dog, to east and
    west,
Expounds the passions burning in
    his breast.
The rising moon o'er that enchanted
    land
Pauses to hear and yearns to
    understand.
                Mowbray Myles.

RIOT, *n.*
A popular entertainment given to the military by innocent bystanders.

R. I. P.
A careless abbreviation of *requiescat in pace*, attesting an indolent goodwill to the dead. According to the learned Dr. Drigge, however, the letters originally meant nothing more than *reductus in pulvis*.

RITE, *n.*
A religious or semi-religious ceremony fixed by law, precept or custom, with the essential oil of sincerity carefully squeezed out of it.

RITUALISM, *n.*
A Dutch Garden of God where He may walk in rectilinear freedom, keeping off the grass.

ROAD, *n.*
A strip of land along which one may pass from where it is too tiresome to be to where it is futile to go.

> All roads, howsoe'er they diverge,
>   lead to Rome,
> Whence, thank the good Lord, at
>   least one leads back home.
> *Borey the Bald.*

ROBBER, *n.*
A candid man of affairs.

It is related of Voltaire that one night he and some traveling companions lodged at a wayside inn. The surroundings were suggestive, and after supper they agreed to tell robber stories in turn. When Voltaire's turn came he said: "Once there was a Farmer-General of the Revenues." Saying nothing more, he was encouraged to continue. "That," he said, "is the story."

ROMANCE, *n.*
Fiction that owes no allegiance to the God of Things as They Are. In the novel the writer's thought is tethered to probability, as a domestic horse to the hitching-post, but in romance it ranges at will over the entire region of the imagination—free, lawless, immune to bit and rein. Your novelist is a poor creature, as Carlyle might say—a mere reporter. He may invent his characters and plot, but he must not imagine anything taking place that might not occur, albeit his entire narrative is candidly a lie. Why he imposes this hard condition on himself, and "drags at each remove a lengthening chain" of his own forging he can explain in ten thick volumes without illuminating by so much as a candle's ray the black profound of his own ignorance of the matter. There are great novels, for great writers have "laid waste their powers" to write them, but it remains true that far and away the most fascinating fiction that we have is "The Thousand and One Nights."

ROPE, *n.*
An obsolescent appliance for reminding assassins that they too are mortal. It is put about the neck and remains in place one's whole life long. It has been largely superseded by a more complex electrical device worn upon another part of the person; and this is rapidly giving place to an apparatus known as the preachment.

ROSTRUM, *n.*
In Latin, the beak of a bird or the prow of a ship. In America, a place from which a candidate for office energetically expounds the wisdom, virtue and power of the rabble.

ROUNDHEAD, *n.*
A member of the Parliamentarian party in the English civil war—so

ROMANCE

called from his habit of wearing his hair short, whereas his enemy, the Cavalier, wore his long. There were other points of difference between them, but the fashion in hair was the fundamental cause of quarrel. The Cavaliers were royalists because the king, an indolent fellow, found it more convenient to let his hair grow than to wash his neck. This the Roundheads, who were mostly barbers and soap-boilers, deemed an injury to trade, and the royal neck was therefore the object of their particular indignation. Descendants of the belligerents now wear their hair all alike, but the fires of animosity enkindled in that ancient strife smoulder to this day beneath the snows of British civility.

RUBBISH, *n.*
Worthless matter, such as the religions, philosophies, literatures, arts and sciences of the tribes infesting the regions lying due south from Boreaplas.

RUIN, *v.*
To destroy. Specifically, to destroy a maid's belief in the virtue of maids.

RUM, *n.*
Generically, fiery liquors that produce madness in total abstainers.

RUMOR, *n.*
A favorite weapon of the assassins of character.

> Sharp, irresistible by mail or shield,
>   By guard unparried as by flight unstayed,
> O serviceable Rumor, let me wield
>   Against my enemy no other blade.
> His be the terror of a foe unseen,
>   His the inutile hand upon the hilt,
> And mine the deadly tongue, long, slender, keen,
>   Hinting a rumor of some ancient guilt.
> So shall I slay the wretch without a blow,
> Spare me to celebrate his overthrow,
> And nurse my valor for another foe.
>   *Joel Buxter.*

RUSSIAN, *n.*
A person with a Caucasian body and a Mongolian soul. A Tartar Emetic.

RUIN

S

SABBATH, *n.*
A weekly festival having its origin in the fact that God made the world in six days and was arrested on the seventh. Among the Jews observance of the day was enforced by a Commandment of which this is the Christian version: "Remember the seventh day to make thy neighbor keep it wholly." To the Creator it seemed fit and expedient that the Sabbath should be the last day of the week, but the Early Fathers of the Church held other views. So great is the sanctity of the day that even where the Lord holds a doubtful and precarious jurisdiction over those who go down to (and down into) the sea it is reverently recognized, as is manifest in the following deepwater version of the Fourth Commandment:

> Six days shalt thou labor and do all
>   thou art able,
> And on the seventh holystone the
>   deck and scrape the cable.

Decks are no longer holystoned, but the cable still supplies the captain with opportunity to attest a pious respect for the divine ordinance.

SACERDOTALIST, *n.*
One who holds the belief that a clergyman is a priest. Denial of this momentous doctrine is the hardiest challenge that is now flung into the teeth of the Episcolopian church by the Neo-Dictionarians.

SACRAMENT, *n.*
A solemn religious ceremony to which several degrees of authority and significance are attached. Rome has seven sacraments, but the Protestant churches, being less prosperous, feel that they can afford only two, and these of inferior sanctity. Some of the smaller sects have no sacraments at all — for which mean economy they will indubitably be damned.

SACRED

SACRED, *adj.*
Dedicated to some religious purpose; having a divine character; inspiring solemn thoughts or emotions; as, the Dalai Lama of Thibet; the Moogum of M'bwango; the temple of Apes in Ceylon; the Cow in India; the Crocodile, the Cat and the Onion of ancient Egypt; the Mufti of Moosh; the hair of the dog that bit Noah, etc.

> All things are either sacred or
>   profane.
> The former to ecclesiasts bring gain;
> The latter to the devil appertain.
>   *Dumbo Omohundro.*

SANDLOTTER, *n.*
A vertebrate mammal holding the political views of Denis Kearney, a notorious demagogue of San Francisco, whose audiences gathered in the open spaces (sandlots) of the town. True to the traditions of his species, this leader of the proletariat was finally bought off by his law-and-order enemies, living prosperously silent and dying impenitently rich. But before his treason he imposed upon California a constitution that was a confection of sin in a diction of solecisms. The similarity between the words "sandlotter" and "sansculotte" is problematically significant, but indubitably suggestive.

SAFETY-CLUTCH, *n.*
A mechanical device acting
automatically to prevent the fall of
an elevator, or cage, in case of an
accident to the hoisting apparatus.

> Once I seen a human ruin
>   In a elevator-well,
> And his members was bestrewin'
>   All the place where he had fell.
>
> And I says, apostrophisin'
>   That uncommon woful wreck:
> "Your position's so surprisin'
>   That I tremble for your neck!"
>
> Then that ruin, smilin' sadly
>   And impressive, up and spoke:
> "Well, I wouldn't tremble badly,
>   For it's been a fortnight broke."
>
> Then, for further comprehension
>   Of his attitude, he begs
> I will focus my attention
>   On his various arms and legs—
>
> How they all are contumacious;
>   Where they each, respective, lie;
> How one trotter proves ungracious,
>   T'other one an *alibi.*
>
> These particulars is mentioned
>   For to show his dismal state,
> Which I wasn't first intentioned
>   To specifical relate.
>
> None is worser to be dreaded
>   That I ever have heard tell
> Than the gent's who there was
>   spreaded
>   In that elevator-well.
>
> Now this tale is allegoric—
>   It is figurative all,
> For the well is metaphoric
>   And the feller didn't fall.
>
> I opine it isn't moral
>   For a writer-man to cheat,
> And despise to wear a laurel
>   As was gotten by deceit.
>
> For 'tis Politics intended
>   By the elevator, mind,
> It will boost a person splendid
>   If his talent is the kind.
>
> Col. Bryan had the talent
>   (For the busted man is him)
> And it shot him up right gallant
>   Till his head begun to swim.
>
> Then the rope it broke above him
>   And he painful come to earth
> Where there's nobody to love him
>   For his detrimented worth.
>
> Though he's livin' none would know
>   him,
>   Or at leastwise not as such.
> Moral of this woful poem:
>   Frequent oil your safety-clutch.
>   *Porfer Poog.*

SAINT, *n.*
A dead sinner revised and edited.

The Duchess of Orleans relates
that the irreverent old calumniator,
Marshal Villeroi, who in his youth
had known St. Francis de Sales,
said, on hearing him called saint: "I
am delighted to hear that Monsieur
de Sales is a saint. He was fond of
saying indelicate things, and used
to cheat at cards. In other respects
he was a perfect gentleman, though
a fool."

SALACITY, *n.*
A certain literary quality
frequently observed in popular
novels, especially in those written
by women and young girls, who
give it another name and think that
in introducing it they are occupying
a neglected field of letters and
reaping an overlooked harvest. If
they have the misfortune to live
long enough they are tormented
with a desire to burn their sheaves.

SALAMANDER, *n.*
Originally a reptile inhabiting fire;
later, an anthropomorphous
immortal, but still a pyrophile.
Salamanders are now believed to be
extinct, the last one of which we
have an account having been seen
in Carcassonne by the Abbé Belloc,
who exorcised it with a bucket of
holy water.

SARCOPHAGUS, *n.*
Among the Greeks a coffin which
being made of a certain kind of
carnivorous stone, had the peculiar
property of devouring the body

placed in it. The sarcophagus known to modern obsequiographers is commonly a product of the carpenter's art.

SATAN, *n.*
One of the Creator's lamentable mistakes, repented in sashcloth and axes. Being instated as an archangel, Satan made himself multifariously objectionable and was finally expelled from Heaven. Halfway in his descent he paused, bent his head in thought a moment and at last went back. "There is one favor that I should like to ask," said he.

"Name it."

"Man, I understand, is about to be created. He will need laws."

"What, wretch! you his appointed adversary, charged from the dawn of eternity with hatred of his soul — you ask for the right to make his laws?"

"Pardon; what I have to ask is that he be permitted to make them himself."

It was so ordered.

SATIETY, *n.*
The feeling that one has for the plate after he has eaten its contents, madam.

SATIRE, *n.*
An obsolete kind of literary composition in which the vices and follies of the author's enemies were expounded with imperfect tenderness. In this country satire never had more than a sickly and uncertain existence, for the soul of it is wit, wherein we are dolefully deficient, the humor that we mistake for it, like all humor, being tolerant and sympathetic. Moreover, although Americans are "endowed by their Creator" with abundant vice and folly, it is not generally known that these are reprehensible qualities, wherefore the satirist is popularly regarded as

a sour-spirited knave, and his every victim's outcry for codefendants evokes a national assent.

SATYR, *n.*
One of the few characters of the Grecian mythology accorded recognition in the Hebrew. (Leviticus, xvii, 7.) The satyr was at first a member of the dissolute community acknowledging a loose allegiance to Dionysius, but underwent many transformations and improvements. Not infrequently he is confounded with the faun, a later and decenter creation of the Romans, who was less like a man and more like a goat.

SATYR

SAUCE, *n.*

The one infallible sign of civilization and enlightenment. A people with no sauces has one thousand vices; a people with one sauce has only nine hundred and ninety-nine. For every sauce invented and accepted a vice is renounced and forgiven.

SAW, *n.*

A trite popular saying, or proverb. (Figurative and colloquial.) So called because it makes its way into a wooden head. Following are examples of old saws fitted with new teeth.

A penny saved is a penny to squander.

A man is known by the company that he organizes.

A bad workman quarrels with the man who calls him that.

A bird in the hand is worth what it will bring.

Better late than before anybody has invited you.

Example is better than following it.

Half a loaf is better than a whole one if there is much else.

Think twice before you speak to a friend in need.

What is worth doing is worth the trouble of asking somebody to do it.

Least said is soonest disavowed.

He laughs best who laughs least.

Speak of the Devil and he will hear about it.

Of two evils choose to be the least.

Strike while your employer has a big contract.

SCARABAEUS, *n.*

The sacred beetle of the ancient Egyptians, allied to our familiar "tumble-bug." It was supposed to symbolize immortality, the fact that God knew why giving it its peculiar sanctity. Its habit of incubating its eggs in a ball of ordure may also have commended it to the favor of the priesthood, and may some day assure it an equal reverence among ourselves. True, the American beetle is an inferior beetle, but the American priest is an inferior priest.

SCARABEE, *n.*

The same as scarabaeus.

> He fell by his own hand
> Beneath the great oak tree.
> He'd traveled in a foreign land.
> He tried to make her understand
> The dance that's called the
> Saraband,
> But he called it Scarabee.
> He had called it so through an
> afternoon,
> And she, the light of his harem if so
> might be,
> Had smiled and said naught. O the
> body was fair to see,
> All frosted there in the shine o' the
> moon—
> Dead for a Scarabee
> And a recollection that came too late.
> O Fate!
> They buried him where he lay,
> He sleeps awaiting the Day,
> In state,
> And two Possible Puns, moon-eyed and
> wan,
> Gloom over the grave and then move
> on.
> Dead for a Scarabee!
> *Fernando Tapple.*

SCARIFICATION, *n.*

A form of penance practised by the mediaeval pious. The rite was performed, sometimes with a knife, sometimes with a hot iron, but always, says Arsenius Asceticus, acceptably if the penitent spared himself no pain nor harmless disfigurement. Scarification, with other crude penances, has now been superseded by benefaction. The

SCEPTER

founding of a library or endowment
of a university is said to yield to the
penitent a sharper and more lasting
pain than is conferred by the knife
or iron, and is therefore a surer
means of grace. There are,
however, two grave objections to it
as a penitential method: the good
that it does and the taint of justice.

SCEPTER, *n.*
A king's staff of office, the sign and
symbol of his authority. It was
originally a mace with which the
sovereign admonished his jester and
vetoed ministerial measures by

breaking the bones of their
proponents.

SCIMITAR, *n.*
A curved sword of exceeding
keenness, in the conduct of which
certain Orientals attain a
surprising proficiency, as the
incident here related will serve to
show. The account is translated
from the Japanese of Shusi Itama, a
famous writer of the thirteenth
century.

When the great Gichi-Kuktai was
Mikado he condemned to decapitation
Jijiji Ri, a high officer of the Court. Soon
after the hour appointed for
performance of the rite what was his
Majesty's surprise to see calmly
approaching the throne the man who
should have been at that time ten
minutes dead!

"Seventeen hundred impossible
dragons!" shouted the enraged monarch.
"Did I not sentence you to stand in the
market-place and have your head struck
off by the public executioner at three
o'clock? And is it not now 3:10?"

"Son of a thousand illustrious deities,"
answered the condemned minister, "all
that you say is so true that the truth is a
lie in comparison. But your heavenly
Majesty's sunny and vitalizing wishes
have been pestilently disregarded. With
joy I ran and placed my unworthy body
in the market-place. The executioner
appeared with his bare scimetar,
ostentatiously whirled it in air, and then,
tapping me lightly upon the neck, strode
away, pelted by the populace, with
whom I was ever a favorite. I am come to
pray for justice upon his own
dishonorable and treasonous head."

"To what regiment of executioners
does the black-boweled caitiff belong?"
asked the Mikado.

"To the gallant Ninety-eight Hundred
and Thirty-seventh—I know the man.
His name is Sakko-Samshi."

"Let him be brought before me," said
the Mikado to an attendant, and a half-
hour later the culprit stood in the
Presence.

"Thou bastard son of a three-legged
hunchback without thumbs!" roared the
sovereign—"why didst thou but lightly
tap the neck that it should have been thy
pleasure to sever?"

"Lord of Cranes and Cherry Blooms,"
replied the executioner, unmoved,

"command him to blow his nose with his fingers."

Being commanded, Jijiji Ri laid hold of his nose and trumpeted like an elephant, all expecting to see the severed head flung violently from him. Nothing occurred: the performance prospered peacefully to the close, without incident.

All eyes were now turned on the executioner, who had grown as white as the snows on the summit of Fujiama. His legs trembled and his breath came in gasps of terror.

"Several kinds of spike-tailed brass lions!" he cried; "I am a ruined and disgraced swordsman! I struck the villain feebly because in flourishing the scimitar I had accidentally passed it through my own neck! Father of the Moon, I resign my office."

So saying, he grasped his top-knot, lifted off his head, and advancing to the throne laid it humbly at the Mikado's feet. .

SCRAP-BOOK, *n.*
A book that is commonly edited by a fool. Many persons of some small distinction compile scrap-books containing whatever they happen to read about themselves or employ others to collect. One of these egotists was addressed in the lines following, by Agamemnon Melancthon Peters:

> Dear Frank, that scrap-book where you boast
> You keep a record true
> Of every kind of peppered roast
> That's made of you;
>
> Wherein you paste the printed gibes
> That revel round your name,
> Thinking the laughter of the scribes
> Attests your fame;
>
> Where all the pictures you arrange
> That comic pencils trace —
> Your funny figure and your strange
> Semitic face —
>
> Pray lend it me. Wit I have not,
> Nor art, but there I'll list
> The daily drubbings you'd have got
> Had God a fist.

SCRIBBLER, *n.*
A professional writer whose views are antagonistic to one's own.

SCRIPTURES, *n.*
The sacred books of our holy religion, as distinguished from the false and profane writings on which all other faiths are based.

SEAL, *n.*
A mark impressed upon certain kinds of documents to attest their authenticity and authority. Sometimes it is stamped upon wax, and attached to the paper, sometimes into the paper itself. Sealing, in this sense, is a survival of an ancient custom of inscribing important papers with cabalistic words or signs to give them a magical efficacy independent of the authority that they represent. In the British museum are preserved many ancient papers, mostly of a sacerdotal character, validated by necromantic pentagrams and other devices, frequently initial letters of words to conjure with; and in many instances these are attached in the same way that seals are appended now. As nearly every reasonless and apparently meaningless custom, rite or observance of modern times had origin in some remote utility, it is pleasing to note an example of ancient nonsense evolving in the process of ages into something really useful. Our word "sincere" is derived from *sine cero*, without wax, but the learned are not in agreement as to whether this refers to the absence of the cabalistic signs, or to that of the wax with which letters were formerly closed from public scrutiny. Either view of the matter will serve one in immediate need of an hypothesis. The initials L. S., commonly appended to signatures of legal documents, mean *locum sigillis*, the place of the seal, although the seal is no longer used — an admirable example of conservatism distinguishing Man from the beasts that perish. The words *locum sigillis* are humbly suggested as a suitable motto for the Pribyloff Islands whenever they shall take their place as a sovereign State of the American Union.

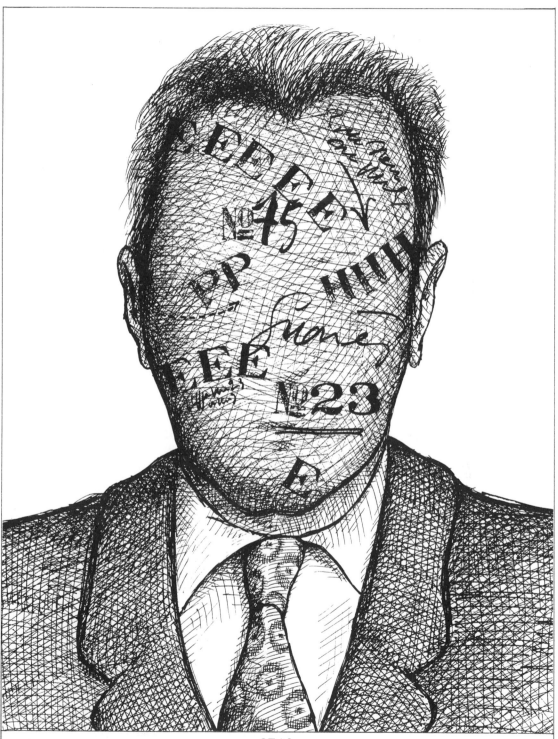

SEAL

SEINE, *n.*

A kind of net for effecting an involuntary change of environment. For fish it is made strong and coarse, but women are more easily taken with a singularly delicate fabric weighted with small, cut stones.

> The devil casting a seine of lace,
>   (With precious stones 'twas
>   weighted)
> Drew it into the landing place
> And its contents calculated.
>
> All souls of women were in that
>   sack—
>   A draft miraculous, precious!
> But ere he could throw it across his
>   back
> They'd all escaped through the
>   meshes.
>   *Baruch de Loppis.*

SELF-ESTEEM, *n.*

An erroneous appraisement.

SELF-EVIDENT, *adj.*

Evident to one's self and to nobody else.

SERIAL, *n.*

A literary work, usually a story that is not true, creeping through several issues of a newspaper or magazine. Frequently appended to each instalment is a "synopsis of preceding chapters" for those who have not read them, but a direr need is a synopsis of succeeding chapters for those who do not intend to read *them*. A synopsis of the entire work would be still better.

The late James F. Bowman was writing a serial tale for a weekly paper in collaboration with a genius whose name has not come down to us. They wrote, not jointly but alternately, Bowman supplying the instalment for one week, his friend for the next, and so on, world without end, they hoped. Unfortunately they quarreled, and one Monday morning when Bowman read the paper to prepare himself for his task, he found his work cut out for him in a way to surprise and pain him. His collaborator had embarked every character of the narrative on a ship and sunk them all in the deepest part of the Atlantic.

SEVERALTY, *n.*

Separateness, as, lands in severalty, *i.e.*, lands held individually, not in joint ownership. Certain tribes of Indians are believed now to be sufficiently civilized to have in severalty the lands that they have hitherto held as tribal organizations, and could not sell to the Whites for waxen beads and potato whiskey.

SELF-ESTEEM

SHERIFF, *n.*
In America the chief executive officer of a county, whose most characteristic duties, in some of the Western and Southern States, are the catching and hanging of rogues.

> John Elmer Pettibone Cajee
> (I write of him with little glee)
> Was just as bad as he could be.
>
> 'Twas frequently remarked: "I swon!
> The sun has never looked upon
> So bad a man as Neighbor John."
>
> A sinner through and through, he
>   had
> This added fault: it made him mad
> To know another man was bad.
>
> In such a case he thought it right
> To rise at any hour of night
> And quench that wicked person's
>   light.
>
> Despite the town's entreaties, he
> Would hale him to the nearest tree
> And leave him swinging wide and
>   free.
>
> Or sometimes, if the humor came,
> A luckless wight's reluctant frame
> Was given to the cheerful flame.
>
> While it was turning nice and
>   brown,
> All unconcerned John met the frown
> Of that austere and righteous town.
>
> "How sad," his neighbors said, "that
>   he
> So scornful of the law should be—
> An anar c, h, i, s, t."
>
> (That is the way that they preferred
> To utter the abhorrent word,
> So strong the aversion that it
>   stirred.)
>
> "Resolved," they said, continuing,
> "That Badman John must cease this
>   thing
> Of having his unlawful fling.
>
> "Now, by these sacred relics"—here
> Each man had out a souvenir
> Got at a lynching yesteryear—
>
> "By these we swear he shall forsake
> His ways, nor cause our hearts to
>   ache
> By sins of rope and torch and stake.
>
> "We'll tie his red right hand until
> He'll have small freedom to fulfil
> The mandates of his lawless will."
>
> So, in convention then and there,
> They named him Sheriff. The affair
> Was opened, it is said, with prayer.
>   *J. Milton Sloluck.*

SIREN, *n.*
One of several musical prodigies famous for a vain attempt to dissuade Odysseus from a life on the ocean wave. Figuratively, any lady of splendid promise, dissembled purpose and disappointing performance.

SLANG, *n.*
The grunt of the human hog (*Pignoramus intolerabilis)* with an audible memory. The speech of one who utters with his tongue what he thinks with his ear, and feels the pride of a creator in accomplishing the feat of a parrot. A means (under Providence) of setting up as a wit without a capital of sense.

SMITHAREEN, *n.*
A fragment, a decomponent part, a remain. The word is used variously, but in the following verses on a noted female reformer who opposed bicycle-riding by women because it "led them to the devil" it is seen at its best:

> The wheels go round without a
>   sound—
>   The maidens hold high revel;
> In sinful mood, insanely gay,
> True spinsters spin adown the way
>   From duty to the devil!
> They laugh, they sing, and—ting-a-
>   ling!
>   Their bells go all the morning;
> Their lanterns bright bestar the
>   night
>   Pedestrians a-warning.

With lifted hands Miss Charlotte
    stands,
  Good-Lording and O-mying,
Her rheumatism forgotten quite,
  Her fat with anger frying.
She blocks the path that leads to
    wrath,
  Jack Satan's power defying.
The wheels go round without a
    sound
  The lights burn red and blue and
    green.
What's this that's found upon the
    ground?
  Poor Charlotte Smith's a
    smithareen!
          John William Yope.

SOPHISTRY, *n.*

The controversial method of an
opponent, distinguished from one's
own by superior insincerity and
fooling. This method is that of the
later Sophists, a Grecian sect of
philosophers who began by teaching
wisdom, prudence, science, art and,
in brief, whatever men ought to
know, but lost themselves in a maze
of quibbles and a fog of words.

  His bad opponent's "facts" he sweeps
    away,
  And drags his sophistry to light of
    day;
  Then swears they're pushed to
    madness who resort
  To falsehood of so desperate a sort.
  Not so; like sods upon a dead man's
    breast,
  He lies most lightly who the least is
    pressed.
          Polydore Smith.

SORCERY, *n.*

The ancient prototype and
forerunner of political influence. It
was, however, deemed less
respectable and sometimes was
punished by torture and death.
Augustine Nicholas relates that a
poor peasant who had been accused
of sorcery was put to the torture to
compel a confession. After enduring
a few gentle agonies the suffering
simpleton admitted his guilt, but
naively asked his tormentors if it
were not possible to be a sorcerer
without knowing it.

SOUL, *n.*

A spiritual entity concerning which
there hath been brave disputation.
Plato held that those souls which in
a previous state of existence
(antedating Athens) had obtained
the clearest glimpses of eternal
truth entered into the bodies of
persons who became philosophers.
Plato was himself a philosopher.
The souls that had least
contemplated divine truth animated
the bodies of usurpers and despots.
Dionysius I, who had threatened to
decapitate the broad-browed
philosopher, was a usurper and
despot. Plato, doubtless, was not the
first to construct a system of
philosophy that could be quoted
against his enemies; certainly he
was not the last.

"Concerning the nature of the
soul," saith the renowned author of
Diversiones Sanctorum, "there hath
been hardly more argument than
that of its place in the body. Mine
own belief is that the soul hath her
seat in the abdomen — in which
faith we may discern and interpret
a truth hitherto unintelligible,
namely that the glutton is of all
men most devout. He is said in the
Scripture to 'make a god of his
belly' — why, then, should he not be
pious, having ever his Deity with
him to freshen his faith? Who so
well as he can know the might and
majesty that he shrines? Truly and
soberly, the soul and the stomach
are one Divine Entity; and such
was the belief of Promasius, who
nevertheless erred in denying it
immortality. He had observed that
its visible and material substance
failed and decayed with the rest of
the body after death, but of its
immaterial essence he knew
nothing. This is what we call the
Appetite, and it survives the wreck
and reek of mortality, to be
rewarded or punished in another
world, according to what it hath
demanded in the flesh. The
Appetite whose coarse clamoring
was for the unwholesome viands of
the general market and the public

SOUL

refectory shall be cast into eternal famine, whilst that which firmly though civilly insisted on ortolans, caviare, terrapin, anchovies, *pâtés de foie gras* and all such Christian comestibles shall flesh its spiritual tooth in the souls of them forever and ever, and wreak its divine thirst upon the immortal parts of the rarest and richest wines ever quaffed here below. Such is my religious faith, though I grieve to confess that neither His Holiness the Pope nor His Grace the Archbishop of Canterbury (whom I equally and profoundly revere) will assent to its dissemination."

SPOOKER, *n.*
A writer whose imagination concerns itself with supernatural phenomena, especially the doings of spooks. One of the most illustrious spookers of our time is Mr. William D. Howells, who introduces a well-credentialed reader to as respectable and mannerly a company of spooks as one could wish to meet. To the terror that invests the chairman of a district school board, the Howells ghost adds something of the mystery enveloping a farmer from another township.

STORY, *n.*
A narrative, commonly untrue. The truth of the stories here following has, however, not been successfully impeached.

One evening Mr. Rudolph Block, of New York, found himself seated at dinner alongside Mr. Percival Pollard, the distinguished critic.

"Mr. Pollard," said he, "my book, *The Biography of a Dead Cow,* is published anonymously, but you can hardly be ignorant of its authorship. Yet in reviewing it you speak of it as the work of the Idiot of the Century. Do you think that fair criticism?"

"I am very sorry, sir," replied the critic, amiably, "but it did not occur to me that you really might not wish the public to know who wrote it."

Mr. W. C. Morrow, who used to live in San Jose, California, was addicted to writing ghost stories which made the reader feel as if a stream of lizards, fresh from the ice, were streaking it up his back and hiding in his hair. San Jose was at that time believed to be haunted by the visible spirit of a noted bandit named Vasquez, who had been hanged there. The town was not very well lighted, and it is putting it mildly to say that San Jose was reluctant to be out o' nights. One particularly dark night two gentlemen were abroad in the loneliest spot within the city limits, talking loudly to keep up their courage, when they came upon Mr. J. J. Owen, a well-known journalist.

"Why, Owen," said one, "what brings you here on such a night as this? You told me that this is one of Vasquez' favorite haunts! And you are a believer. Aren't you afraid to be out?"

"My dear fellow," the journalist replied with a drear autumnal cadence in his speech, like the moan of a leaf-laden wind, "I am afraid to be in. I have one of Will Morrow's stories in my pocket and I don't dare to go where there is light enough to read it."

Rear-Admiral Schley and Representative Charles F. Joy were standing near the Peace Monument, in Washington, discussing the question, Is success a failure? Mr. Joy suddenly broke off in the middle of an eloquent sentence, exclaiming: "Hello! I've heard that band before. Santlemann's, I think."

"I don't hear any band," said Schley.

"Come to think, I don't either," said Joy, "but I see General Miles coming down the avenue, and that pageant always affects me in the same way as a brass band. One has to scrutinize one's impressions pretty closely, or one will mistake their origin."

While the Admiral was digesting this hasty meal of philosophy General Miles passed in review, a spectacle of impressive dignity. When the tail of the seeming procession had passed and the two observers had recovered from the transient blindness caused by its effulgence—

"He seems to be enjoying himself," said the Admiral.

"There is nothing," assented Joy, thoughtfully, "that he enjoys one-half so well."

The illustrious statesman, Champ Clark, once lived about a mile from the village of Jebigue, in Missouri. One day he rode into town on a favorite mule, and, hitching the beast on the sunny side of a street, in front of a saloon, he went inside in his character of teetotaler, to apprise the barkeeper that wine is a mocker. It was a dreadfully hot day. Pretty soon a neighbor came in and seeing Clark, said:

"Champ, it is not right to leave that mule out there in the sun. He'll roast, sure!—he was smoking as I passed him."

"O, he's all right," said Clark, lightly; "he's an inveterate smoker."

The neighbor took a lemonade, but shook his head and repeated that it was not right.

He was a conspirator. There had been a fire the night before: a stable just around the corner had burned and a number of horses had put on their immortality, among them a young colt, which was roasted to a rich nut-brown. Some of the boys had turned Mr. Clark's mule loose and substituted the mortal part of the colt. Presently another man entered the saloon.

"For mercy's sake!" he said, taking it with sugar, "do remove that mule, barkeeper: it smells."

"Yes," interposed Clark, "that animal has the best nose in Missouri. But if he doesn't mind,

you shouldn't."

In the course of human events Mr. Clark went out, and there, apparently, lay the incinerated and shrunken remains of his charger. The boys did not have any fun out of Mr. Clark, who looked at the body and, with the non-committal expression to which he owes so much of his political preferment, went away. But walking home late that night he saw his mule standing silent and solemn by the wayside in the misty moonlight. Mentioning the name of Helen Blazes with uncommon emphasis, Mr. Clark took the back track as hard as ever he could hook it, and passed the night in town.

General H. H. Wotherspoon, president of the Army War College, has a pet rib-nosed baboon, an animal of uncommon intelligence but imperfectly beautiful. Returning to his apartment one evening, the General was surprised and pained to find Adam (for so the creature is named, the general being a Darwinian) sitting up for him and wearing its master's best uniform coat, epaulettes and all.

"You confounded remote ancestor!" thundered the great strategist, "what do you mean by being out of bed after taps?—and with my coat on!"

Adam rose and with a reproachful look got down on all fours in the manner of his kind and, scuffling across the room to a table, returned with a visiting-card: General Barry had called and, judging by an empty champagne bottle and several cigar stumps, had been hospitably entertained while waiting. The general apologized to his faithful progenitor and retired. The next day he met General Barry, who said:

"Spoon, old man, when leaving you last evening I forgot to ask you about those excellent cigars. Where do you get them?"

General Wotherspoon did not deign to reply, but walked away.

"Pardon me, please," said Barry, moving after him; "I was joking of course. Why, I knew it was not you before I had been in the room fifteen minutes."

SUCCESS, *n.*
The one unpardonable sin against one's fellows. In literature, and particularly in poetry, the elements of success are exceedingly simple, and are admirably set forth in the following lines by the reverend Father Gassalasca Jape, entitled, for some mysterious reason, "John A. Joyce."

> The bard who would prosper must
>   carry a book,
> Do his thinking in prose and wear
> A crimson cravat, a far-away look
> And a head of hexameter hair.
> Be thin in your thought and your
>   body'll be fat;
> If you wear your hair long you
>   needn't your hat.

SUFFRAGE, *n.*
Expression of opinion by means of a ballot. The right of suffrage (which is held to be both a privilege and a duty) means, as commonly interpreted, the right to vote for the man of another man's choice, and is highly prized. Refusal to do so has the bad name of "incivism." The incivilian, however, cannot be properly arraigned for his crime, for there is no legitimate accuser. If the accuser is himself guilty he has no standing in the court of opinion; if not, he profits by the crime, for A's abstention from voting gives greater weight to the vote of B. By female suffrage is meant the right of a woman to vote as some man tells her to. It is based on female responsibility, which is somewhat limited. The woman most eager to jump out of her petticoat to assert her rights is first to jump back into it when threatened with a switching for misusing them.

SYLPH, *n.*
An immaterial but visible being that inhabited the air when the air was an element and before it was fatally polluted by factory smoke, sewer gas and similar products of civilization. Sylphs were allied to gnomes, nymphs and salamanders, which dwelt, respectively, in earth, water and fire, all now insalubrious. Sylphs, like fowls of the air, were male and female, to no purpose, apparently, for if they had progeny they must have nested in inaccessible places, none of the chicks having ever been seen.

SYMBOL, *n.*
Something that is supposed to typify or stand for something else. Many symbols are mere "survivals"—things which having no longer any utility continue to exist because we have inherited the tendency to make them; as funeral urns carved on memorial monuments. They were once real urns holding the ashes of the dead. We cannot stop making them, but we can give them a name that conceals our helplessness.

SYMBOLIC, *adj.*
Pertaining to symbols and the use and interpretation of symbols.

> They say 'tis conscience feels
>   compunction;
> I hold that that's the stomach's
>   function,
> For of the sinner I have noted
> That when he's sinned he's
>   somewhat bloated,
> Or ill some other ghastly fashion
> Within that bowel of compassion.
> True, I believe the only sinner
> Is he that eats a shabby dinner.
> You know how Adam with good
>   reason,
> For eating apples out of season,
> Was "cursed." But that is all
>   symbolic:
> The truth is, Adam had the colic.
>   *G. J.*

T

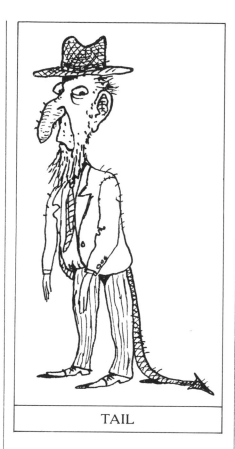

TAIL

TAIL, *n.*
The part of an animal's spine that has transcended its natural limitations to set up an independent existence in a world of its own. Excepting in his foetal state, Man is without a tail, a privation of which he attests an hereditary and uneasy consciousness by the coat-skirt of the male and the train of the female, and by a marked tendency to ornament that part of his attire where the tail should be, and indubitably once was. This tendency is most observable in the female of the species, in whom the ancestral sense is strong and persistent. The tailed men described by Lord Monboddo are now generally regarded as a product of an imagination usually susceptible to influences generated in the golden age of our pithecan past.

TAKE, *v. t.*
To acquire, frequently by force but preferably by stealth.

TALK, *v. t.*
To commit an indiscretion without temptation, from an impulse without purpose.

TARIFF, *n.*
A scale of taxes on imports, designed to protect the domestic producer against the greed of his consumer.

> The enemy of Human Souls
> Sat grieving at the cost of coals;
> For Hell had been annexed of late,
> And was a sovereign Southern State.
>
> "It were no more than right," said
> he,
> "That I should get my fuel free.
> The duty, neither just nor wise,
> Compels me to economize—
> Whereby my broilers, every one,
> Are execrably underdone.
> What would they have?—although I
> yearn
> To do them nicely to a turn,
> I can't afford an honest heat.
> This tariff makes even devils cheat!
> I'm ruined, and my humble trade
> All rascals may at will invade:
> Beneath my nose the public press
> Outdoes me in sulphureousness;
> The bar ingeniously applies
> To my undoing my own lies;
> My medicines the doctors use
> (Albeit vainly) to refuse
> To me my fair and rightful prey
> And keep their own in shape to pay;
> The preachers by example teach
> What, scorning to perform, I preach;
> And statesmen, aping me, all make
> More promises than they can break.
> Against such competition I
> Lift up a disregarded cry.
> Since all ignore my just complaint,
> By Hokey-Pokey! I'll turn saint!"
> Now, the Republicans, who all
> Are saints, began at once to bawl
> Against *his* competition; so
> There was a devil of a go!
> They locked horns with him, tête-a—
> tête
> In acrimonious debate,
> Till Democrats, forlorn and lone,
> Had hopes of coming by their own.
> That evil to avert, in haste

The two belligerents embraced;
But since 'twere wicked to relax
A tittle of the Sacred Tax,
'Twas finally agreed to grant
The bold Insurgent-protestant
A bounty on each soul that fell
Into his ineffectual Hell.

Edam Smith

TECHNICALITY, *n.*
In an English court a man named
Home was tried for slander in
having accused a neighbor of
murder. His exact words were: "Sir
Thomas Holt hath taken a cleaver
and stricken his cook upon the
head, so that one side of the head
fell upon one shoulder and the other
side upon the other shoulder." The
defendant was acquitted by
instruction of the court, the learned
judges holding that the words did
not charge murder, for they did not
affirm the death of the cook, that
being only an inference.

TEDIUM, *n.*
Ennui, the state or condition of one
that is bored. Many fanciful
derivations of the word have been
affirmed, but so high an authority
as Father Jape says that it comes
from a very obvious source—the
first words of the ancient Latin
hymn *Te Deum Laudamus.* In this
apparently natural derivation there
is something that saddens.

TEETOTALER, *n.*
One who abstains from strong
drink, sometimes totally, sometimes
tolerably totally.

TELEPHONE, *n.*
An invention of the devil which
abrogates some of the advantages of
making a disagreeable person keep
his distance.

TELESCOPE, *n.*
A device having a relation to the
eye similar to that of the telephone
to the ear, enabling distant objects
to plague us with a multitude of
needless details. Luckily it is
unprovided with a bell summoning
us to the sacrifice.

TENACITY, *n.*
A certain quality of the human
hand in its relation to the coin of
the realm. It attains its highest
development in the hand of
authority and is considered a
serviceable equipment for a career
in politics. The following
illustrative lines were written of a
Californian gentleman in high
political preferment, who has
passed to his accounting:

Of such tenacity his grip
That nothing from his hand can slip.
Well-buttered eels you may
    o'erwhelm
In tubs of liquid slippery-elm
In vain—from his detaining pinch
They cannot struggle half an inch!
'Tis lucky that he so is planned
That breath he draws not with his
    hand,
For if he did, so great his greed
He'd draw his last with eager speed.
Nay, that were well, you say. Not so
He'd draw but never let it go!

THEOSOPHY, *n.*
An ancient faith having all the
certitude of religion and all the
mystery of science. The modern
Theosophist holds, with the
Buddhists, that we live an
incalculable number of times on
this earth, in as many several
bodies, because one life is not long
enough for our complete spiritual
development; that is, a single
lifetime does not suffice for us to
become as wise and good as we
choose to wish to become. To be
absolutely wise and good—that is
perfection; and the Theosophist is so
keen-sighted as to have observed
that everything desirous of
improvement eventually attains
perfection. Less competent
observers are disposed to except
cats, which seem neither wiser nor
better than they were last year. The
greatest and fattest of recent
Theosophists was the late Madame
Blavatsky, who had no cat.

THEOSOPHY

TIGHTS, *n.*
An habiliment of the stage designed
to reinforce the general acclamation
of the press agent with a particular
publicity. Public attention was once
somewhat diverted from this
garment to Miss Lillian Russell's
refusal to wear it, and many were
the conjectures as to her motive, the
guess of Miss Pauline Hall showing
a high order of ingenuity and
sustained reflection. It was Miss
Hall's belief that nature had not
endowed Miss Russell with
beautiful legs. This theory was
impossible of acceptance by the
male understanding, but the
conception of a faulty female leg
was of so prodigious originality as
to rank among the most brilliant
feats of philosophical speculation! It
is strange that in all the
controversy regarding Miss
Russell's aversion to tights no one
seems to have thought to ascribe it
to what was known among the
ancients as "modesty." The nature
of that sentiment is now
imperfectly understood, and
possibly incapable of exposition
with the vocabulary that remains to
us. The study of lost arts has,
however, been recently revived and
some of the arts themselves
recovered. This is an epoch of
renaissances, and there is ground
for hope that the primitive "blush"
may be dragged from its hiding-
place amongst the tombs of
antiquity and hissed on to the stage.

TOMB, *n.*
The House of Indifference. Tombs
are now by common consent
invested with a certain sanctity, but
when they have been long tenanted
it is considered no sin to break
them open and rifle them, the
famous Egyptologist, Dr. Huggyns,
explaining that a tomb may be
innocently "glened" as soon as its
occupant is done "smellynge," the
soul being then all exhaled. This
reasonable view is now generally
accepted by archaeologists,
whereby the noble science of

Curiosity has been greatly
dignified.

TOPE, *v.*
To tipple, booze, swill, soak, guzzle,
lush, bib, or swig. In the individual,
toping is regarded with disesteem,
but toping nations are in the
forefront of civilization and power.
When pitted against the hard-
drinking Christians the abstemious
Mahometans go down like grass
before the scythe. In India one
hundred thousand beef-eating and
brandy-and-soda guzzling Britons
hold in subjection two hundred and
fifty million vegetarian abstainers
of the same Aryan race. With what
an easy grace the whisky-loving
American pushed the temperate
Spaniard out of his possessions!
From the time when the Berserkers
ravaged all the coasts of western
Europe and lay drunk in every
conquered port it has been the same
way: everywhere the nations that
drink too much are observed to
fight rather well and not too
righteously. Wherefore the
estimable old ladies who abolished
the canteen from the American
army may justly boast of having
materially augmented the nation's
military power.

TREE, *n.*
A tall vegetable intended by nature
to serve as a penal apparatus,
though through a miscarriage of
justice most trees bear only a
negligible fruit, or none at all.
When naturally fruited, the tree is
a beneficent agency of civilization
and an important factor in public
morals. In the stern West and the
sensitive South its fruit (white and
black respectively) though not
eaten, is agreeable to the public
taste and, though not exported,
profitable to the general welfare.
That the legitimate relation of the
tree to justice was no discovery of
Judge Lynch (who, indeed,
conceded it no primacy over the
lamp-post and the bridge-girder) is

made plain by the following passage from Morryster, who antedated him by two centuries:

While in yt londe I was carryed to see ye Ghogo tree, whereof I had hearde moch talk; but sayynge yt I saw naught remarkabyll in it, ye hed manne of ye villayge where it grewe made answer as followeth:
"Ye tree is not nowe in fruite, but in his seasonne you shall see dependynge fr. his braunches all soch as have affroynted ye King his Majesty."
And I was furder tolde yt ye worde "Ghogo" sygnifyeth in yr tong ye same as "rapscal" in our owne. — *Trauvells in ye Easte.*

TREE

TRIAL, *n.*
A formal inquiry designed to prove and put upon record the blameless characters of judges, advocates and jurors. In order to effect this purpose it is necessary to supply a contrast in the person of one who is called the defendant, the prisoner, or the accused. If the contrast is made sufficiently clear this person is made to undergo such an affliction as will give the virtuous gentlemen a comfortable sense of their immunity, added to that of their worth. In our day the accused is usually a human being, or a socialist, but in mediaeval times, animals, fishes, reptiles and insects were brought to trial. A beast that had taken human life, or practiced sorcery, was duly arrested, tried and, if condemned, put to death by the public executioner. Insects ravaging grain fields, orchards or vineyards were cited to appeal by counsel before a civil tribunal, and after testimony, argument and condemnation, if they continued *in contumaciam* the matter was taken to a high ecclesiastical court, where they were solemnly excommuni- cated and anathematized. In a street of Toledo, some pigs that had wickedly run between the viceroy's legs, upsetting him, were arrested on a warrant, tried and punished. In Naples an ass was condemned to be burned at the stake, but the sentence appears not to have been executed. D'Addosio relates from the court records many trials of pigs, bulls, horses, cocks, dogs, goats, etc., greatly, it is believed, to the betterment of their conduct and morals. In 1451 a suit was brought against the leeches infesting some ponds about Berne, and the Bishop of Lausanne, instructed by the faculty of Heidelberg University, directed that some of "the aquatic worms" be brought before the local magistracy. This was done and the leeches, both present and absent, were ordered to leave the places that they had infested within three days on pain of incurring "the malediction of God." In the

voluminous records of this *cause celebre* nothing is found to show whether the offenders braved the punishment, or departed forthwith out of that inhospitable jurisdiction.

TRICHINOSIS, *n.*
The pig's reply to proponents of porcophagy.

Moses Mendlessohn having fallen ill sent for a Christian physician, who at once diagnosed the philosopher's disorder as trichinosis, but tactfully gave it another name. "You need an immediate change of diet," he said; "you must eat six ounces of pork every other day."

"Pork?" shrieked the patient— "pork? Nothing shall induce me to touch it!"

"Do you mean that?" the doctor gravely asked.

"I swear it!"

"Good!—then I will undertake to cure you."

TRINITY, *n.*
In the multiplex theism of certain Christian churches, three entirely distinct deities consistent with only one. Subordinate deities of the polytheistic faith, such as devils and angels, are not dowered with the power of combination, and must urge individually their claims to adoration and propitiation. The Trinity is one of the most sublime mysteries of our holy religion. In rejecting it because it is incomprehensible, Unitarians betray their inadequate sense of theological fundamentals. In religion we believe only what we do not understand, except in the instance of an intelligible doctrine that contradicts an incomprehensible one. In that case we believe the former as a part of the latter.

TROGLODYTE, *n.*
Specifically, a cave-dweller of the paleolithic period, after the Tree

and before the Flat. A famous community of troglodytes dwelt with David in the Cave of Adullam. The colony consisted of "every one that was in distress, and every one that was in debt, and every one that was discontented"—in brief, all the Socialists of Judah.

TRUCE, *n.*
Friendship.

TRUTH, *n.*
An ingenious compound of desirability and appearance. Discovery of truth is the sole purpose of philosophy, which is the most ancient occupation of the human mind and has a fair prospect of existing with increasing activity to the end of time.

TRUTHFUL, *adj.*
Dumb and illiterate.

TRUST, *n.*
In American politics, a large corporation composed in greater part of thrifty working men, widows of small means, orphans in the care of guardians and the courts, with many similar malefactors and public enemies.

TURKEY, *n.*
A large bird whose flesh when eaten on certain religious anniversaries has the peculiar property of attesting piety and gratitude. Incidentally, it is pretty good eating.

TWICE, *adv.*
Once too often.

TYPE, *n.*
Pestilent bits of metal suspected of destroying civilization and enlightenment, despite their obvious agency in this incomparable dictionary.

TRUTH

U

UBIQUITY, *n.*
The gift or power of being in all places at one time, but not in all places at all times, which is omnipresence, an attribute of God and the luminiferous ether only. This important distinction between ubiquity and omnipresence was not clear to the mediaeval Church and there was much bloodshed about it. Certain Lutherans, who affirmed the presence everywhere of Christ's body were known as Ubiquitarians. For this error they were doubtless damned, for Christ's body is present only in the eucharist, though that sacrament may be performed in more than one place simultaneously. In recent times ubiquity has not always been understood — not even by Sir Boyle Roche, for example, who held that a man cannot be in two places at once unless he is a bird.

ULTIMATUM, *n.*
In diplomacy, a last demand before resorting to concessions.

Having received an ultimatum from Austria, the Turkish Ministry met to consider it.

"O servant of the Prophet," said the Sheik of the Imperial Chibouk to the Mamoosh of the Invincible Army, "how many unconquerable soldiers have we in arms?"

"Upholder of the Faith," that dignitary replied after examining his memoranda, "they are in numbers as the leaves of the forest!"

ULTIMATUM

"And how many impenetrable battleships strike terror to the hearts of all Christian swine?" he asked the Imaum of the Ever Victorious Navy.

"Uncle of the Full Moon," was the reply, "deign to know that they are as the waves of the ocean, the sands of the desert and the stars of Heaven!"

For eight hours the broad brow of the Sheik of the Imperial Chibouk was corrugated with evidences of deep thought: he was calculating the chances of war. Then, "Sons of angels," he said, "the die is cast! I shall suggest to the Ulema of the Imperial Ear that he advise inaction. In the name of Allah, the council is adjourned."

UN-AMERICAN, *adj.*
Wicked, intolerable, heathenish.

UNCTION, *n.*
An oiling, or greasing. The rite of extreme unction consists in touching with oil consecrated by a bishop several parts of the body of one engaged in dying. Marbury relates that after the rite had been administered to a certain wicked English nobleman it was discovered that the oil had not been properly consecrated and no other could be obtained. When informed of this the sick man said in anger: "Then I'll be damned if I die!"

"My son," said the priest, "that is what we fear."

UNDERSTANDING, *n.*
A cerebral secretion that enables one having it to know a house from a horse by the roof on the house. Its nature and laws have been exhaustively expounded by Locke, who rode a house, and Kant, who lived in a horse.

His understanding was so keen
That all things which he'd felt, heard, seen,
He could interpret without fail
If he was in or out of jail.
He wrote at Inspiration's call
Deep disquisitions on them all,
Then, pent at last in an asylum,
Performed the service to compile 'em.
So great a writer, all men swore,
They never had not read before.
Jorrock Wormley.

UNITARIAN, *n.*
One who denies the divinity of a Trinitarian.

UNIVERSALIST, *n.*
One who foregoes the advantage of a Hell for persons of another faith.

URBANITY, *n.*
The kind of civility that urban observers ascribe to dwellers in all cities but New York. Its commonest expression is heard in the words, "I beg your pardon," and it is not inconsistent with disregard of the rights of others.

The owner of a powder mill
Was musing on a distant hill—
Something his mind foreboded—
When from the cloudless sky there fell
A deviled human kidney! Well,
The man's mill had exploded.
His hat he lifted from his head;
"I beg your pardon, sir," he said;
"I didn't know 'twas loaded."
Swatkin.

USAGE, *n.*
The First Person of the literary Trinity, the Second and Third being Custom and Conventionality. Imbued with a decent reverence for this Holy Triad an industrious writer may hope to produce books that will live as long as the fashion.

UXORIOUSNESS, *n.*
A perverted affection that has strayed to one's own wife.

V

VOTE

VALOR, *n.*
A soldierly compound of vanity, duty and the gambler's hope.

"Why have you halted?" roared the commander of a division at Chickamauga, who had ordered a charge; "move forward, sir, at once."

"General," said the commander of the delinquent brigade, "I am persuaded that any further display of valor by my troops will bring them into collision with the enemy."

VANITY, *n.*
The tribute of a fool to the worth of the nearest ass.

They say that hens do cackle loudest when
　There's nothing vital in the eggs they've laid;
　And there are hens, professing to have made
A study of mankind, who say that men
Whose business 'tis to drive the tongue or pen
　Make the most clamorous fanfaronade
　O'er their most worthless work; and I'm afraid

They're not entirely different from the hen.
Lo! the drum-major in his coat of gold,
　His blazing breeches and high-towering cap—
Imperiously pompous, grandly bold,
　Grim, resolute, an awe-inspiring chap!
Who'd think this gorgeous creature's only virtue
Is that in battle he will never hurt you?
Hannibal Hunsiker.

VIRTUES, *n. pl.*
Certain abstentions.

VITUPERATION, *n.*
Satire, as understood by dunces and all such as suffer from an impediment in their wit.

VOTE, *n.*
The instrument and symbol of a freeman's power to make a fool of himself and a wreck of his country.

W

W

(double U) has, of all the letters in our alphabet, the only cumbrous name, the names of the others being monosyllabic. This advantage of the Roman alphabet over the Grecian is the more valued after audibly spelling out some simple Greek word, like πιχοριαμβικός. Still, it is now thought by the learned that other agencies than the difference of the two alphabets may have been concerned in the decline of "the glory that was Greece" and the rise of "the grandeur that was Rome." There can be no doubt, however, that by simplifying the name of W (calling it "wow," for example) our civilization could be, if not promoted, at least better endured.

WALL STREET, *n.*

A symbol of sin for every devil to rebuke. That Wall Street is a den of thieves is a belief that serves every unsuccessful thief in place of a hope in Heaven. Even the great and good Andrew Carnegie has made his profession of faith in the matter.

> Carnegie the dauntless has uttered
> his call
> To battle: "The brokers are parasites
> all!"
> Carnegie, Carnegie, you'll never
> prevail;
> Keep the wind of your slogan to
> belly your sail,
> Go back to your isle of perpetual
> brume,
> Silence your pibroch, doff tartan
> and plume:
> Ben Lomond is calling his son from
> the fray —
> Fly, fly from the region of Wall
> Street away!
> While still you're possessed of a
> single baubee
> (I wish it were pledged to
> endowment of me)
> 'Twere wise to retreat from the wars
> of finance
> Lest its value decline ere your credit
> advance.
> For a man 'twixt a king of finance
> and the sea,
> Carnegie, Carnegie, your tongue is
> too free!
>
> *Anonymus Bink.*

WAR

WAR, *n.*

A by-product of the arts of peace. The most menacing political condition is a period of international amity. The student of history who has not been taught to expect the unexpected may justly boast himself inaccessible to the light. "In time of peace prepare for war" has a deeper meaning than is commonly discerned; it means, not merely that all things earthly have an end — that change is the one immutable and eternal law — but that the soil of peace is thickly sown with seeds of war and singularly suited to their germination and growth. It was when Kubla Khan had decreed his "stately pleasure dome" — when, that is to say, there were peace and fat feasting in Xanadu — that he

> heard from far
> Ancestral voices prophesying war.

One of the greatest of poets, Coleridge was one of the wisest of men, and it was not for nothing that he read us this parable. Let us have a little less of "hands across the sea," and a little more of that elemental distrust that is the security of nations. War loves to come like a thief in the night; professions of eternal amity provide the night.

WASHINGTONIAN, *n.*
A Potomac tribesman who exchanged the privilege of governing himself for the advantage of good government. In justice to him it should be said that he did not want to.

> They took away his vote and gave
>   instead
> The right, when he had earned, to
>   *eat* his bread.
> In vain—he clamors for his "boss,"
>   poor soul,
> To come again and part him from
>   his roll.
>   *Offenbach Stutz.*

WEAKNESSES, *n. pl.*
Certain primal powers of Tyrant Woman wherewith she holds dominion over the male of her species, binding him to the service of her will and paralyzing his rebellious energies.

WEATHER, *n.*
The climate of an hour. A permanent topic of conversation among persons whom it does not interest, but who have inherited the tendency to chatter about it from naked arboreal ancestors whom it keenly concerned. The setting up of official weather bureaus and their maintenance in mendacity prove that even governments are accessible to suasion by the rude forefathers of the jungle.

> Once I dipt into the future far as
>   human eye could see,
> And I saw the Chief Forecaster, dead
>   as any one can be—

> Dead and damned and shut in Hades
>   as a liar from his birth,
> With a record of unreason seldom
>   paralleled on earth.
> While I looked he reared him
>   solemnly, that incandescent youth,
> From the coals that he'd preferred to
>   the advantages of truth.
> He cast his eyes about him and above
>   him; then he wrote
> On a slab of thin asbestos what I
>   venture here to quote—
> For I read it in the rose-light of the
>   everlasting glow:
> "Cloudy; variable winds, with local
>   showers; cooler; snow."
>   *Halcyon Jones.*

WEDDING, *n.*
A ceremony at which two persons undertake to become one, one undertakes to become nothing, and nothing undertakes to become supportable.

WEREWOLF, *n.*
A wolf that was once, or is sometimes, a man. All werewolves are of evil disposition, having assumed a bestial form to gratify a bestial appetite, but some, transformed by sorcery, are as humane as is consistent with an acquired taste for human flesh.

Some Bavarian peasants having caught a wolf one evening, tied it to a post by the tail and went to bed. The next morning nothing was there! Greatly perplexed, they consulted the local priest, who told them that their captive was undoubtedly a werewolf and had resumed its human form during the night. "The next time that you take a wolf," the good man said, "see that you chain it by the leg, and in the morning you will find a Lutheran."

WHANGDEPOOTENAWAH, *n.*
In the Ojibwa tongue, disaster; an unexpected affliction that strikes hard.

> Should you ask me whence this
>   laughter,

Whence this audible big-smiling,
With its labial extension,
With its maxillar distortion
And its diaphragmic rhythmus
Like the billowing of ocean,
Like the shaking of a carpet,
I should answer, I should tell you:
From the great deeps of the spirit,
From the unplummeted abysmus
Of the soul this laughter welleth
As the fountain, the gug-guggle,
Like the river from the cañon,
To entoken and give warning
That my present mood is sunny.
Should you ask me further
    question —
Why the great deeps of the spirit,
Why the unplummeted abysmus
Of the soul extrudes this laughter,
This all audible big-smiling,
I should answer, I should tell you
With a white heart, tumpitumpy,
With a true tongue, honest Injun:
William Bryan, he has Caught It,
Caught the Whangdepootenawah!

Is't the sandhill crane, the shankank,
Standing in the marsh, the
    kneedeep,
Standing silent in the kneedeep
With his wing-tips crossed behind
    him
And his neck close-reefed before
    him,
With his bill, his william, buried
In the down upon his bosom,
With his head retracted inly,
While his shoulders overlook it?
Does the sandhill crane, the
    shankank,
Shiver grayly in the north wind,
Wishing he had died when little,
As the sparrow, the chipchip, does?
No 'tis not the Shankank standing,
Standing in the gray and dismal
Marsh, the gray and dismal
    kneedeep.
No, 'tis peerless William Bryan
Realizing that he's Caught It,
Caught the Whangdepootenawah!

WHEAT, *n.*
A cereal from which a tolerably
good whisky can with some
difficulty be made, and which is
used also for bread. The French are
said to eat more bread *per capita* of
population than any other people,
which is natural, for only they
know how to make the stuff
palatable.

WHITE, *adj.* and *n.*
Black.

WIDOW, *n.*
A pathetic figure that the Christian
world has agreed to take
humorously, although Christ's
tenderness toward widows was one
of the most marked features of his
character.

WINE, *n.*
Fermented grape-juice known to
the Women's Christian Union as
"liquor," sometimes as "rum." Wine,
madam, is God's next best gift to
man.

WIT, *n.*
The salt with which the American
humorist spoils his intellectual
cookery by leaving it out.

WITCH, *n.*
(1) An ugly and repulsive old
woman, in a wicked league with the
devil. (2) A beautiful and attractive
young woman, in wickedness a
league beyond the devil.

WITCH

WITTICISM, *n.*
A sharp and clever remark, usually quoted, and seldom noted; what the Philistine is pleased to call a "joke."

WOMAN, *n.*
An animal usually living in the vicinity of Man, and having a rudimentary susceptibility to domestication. It is credited by many of the elder zoologists with a certain vestigial docility acquired in a former state of seclusion, but naturalists of the postsusananthony period, having no knowledge of the seclusion, deny the virtue and declare that such as creation's dawn beheld, it roareth now. The species is the most widely distributed of all beasts of prey, infesting all habitable parts of the globe, from Greenland's spicy mountains to India's moral strand. The popular name (wolfman) is incorrect, for the creature is of the cat kind. The woman is lithe and graceful in its movements, especially the American variety *(Felis pugnans)*, is omnivorous and can be taught not to talk. —*Balthasar Pober.*

WORMS'-MEAT, *n.*
The finished product of which we are the raw material. The contents of the Taj Mahal, the Tombeau Napoleon and the Grantarium. Worms'-meat is usually outlasted by the structure that houses it, but "this too must pass away." Probably the silliest work in which a human being can engage is construction of a tomb for himself. The solemn purpose cannot dignify, but only accentuates by contrast the foreknown futility.

> Ambitious fool! so mad to be a show!
> How profitless the labor you bestow
>   Upon a dwelling whose
>   magnificence
> The tenant neither can admire nor
>   know.
>
> Build deep, build high, build
>   massive as you can,

The wanton grass-roots will defeat
  the plan
By shouldering asunder all the
  stones
In what to you would be a moment's
  span.

Time to the dead so all unreckoned
  flies
That when your marble all is dust,
  arise,
  If wakened, stretch your limbs
    and yawn —
You'll think you scarcely can have
  closed your eyes.

What though of all man's works
  your tomb alone
Should stand till Time himself be
  overthrown?
  Would it advantage you to dwell
    therein
Forever as a stain upon a stone?
                    Joel Huck.

WORSHIP, *n.*
Homo Creator's testimony to the sound construction and fine finish of Deus Creatus. A popular form of abjection, having an element of pride.

WRATH, *n.*
Anger of a superior quality and degree, appropriate to exalted characters and momentous occasions; as, "the wrath of God," "the day of wrath," etc. Amongst the ancients the wrath of kings was deemed sacred, for it could usually command the agency of some god for its fit manifestation, as could also that of a priest. The Greeks before Troy were so harried by Apollo that they jumped out of the frying-pan of the wrath of Chryses into the fire of the wrath of Achilles, though Agamemnon, the sole offender, was neither fried nor roasted. A similar noted immunity was that of David when he incurred the wrath of Yahveh by numbering his people, seventy thousand of whom paid the penalty with their lives. God is now Love, and a director of the census performs his work without apprehension of disaster.

X

X
in our alphabet being a needless letter has an added invincibility to the attacks of the spelling reformers, and like them, will doubtless last as long as the language. X is the sacred symbol of ten dollars, and in such words as Xmas, Xn, etc., stands for Christ, not, as is popularly supposed, because it represents a cross, but because the corresponding letter in the Greek alphabet is the initial of his name—Χριστός. If it represented a cross it would stand for St. Andrew, who "testified" upon one of that shape. In the algebra of psychology x stands for Woman's mind. Words beginning with X are Grecian and will not be defined in this standard English dictionary.

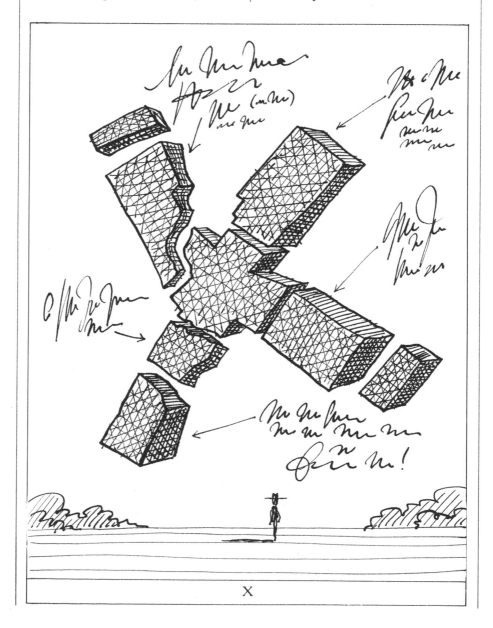

X

Y

YANKEE, *n.*
In Europe, an American. In the Northern States of our Union, a New Englander. In the Southern States the word is unknown. (See DAMYANK.)

YEAR, *n.*
A period of three hundred and sixty-five disappointments.

YESTERDAY, *n.*
The infancy of youth, the youth of manhood, the entire past of age.

But yesterday I should have thought
  me blest
    To stand high-pinnacled upon the
    peak
    Of middle life and look adown the
    bleak
And unfamiliar foreslope to the
  West,
Where solemn shadows all the land
  invest
    And stilly voices, half-
    remembered, speak
    Unfinished prophecy, and witch-
    fires freak
The haunted twilight of the Dark of
  Rest.
Yea, yesterday my soul was all
  aflame
    To stay the shadow on the dial's
    face
At manhood's noonmark! Now, in
  God His name
    I chide aloud the little interspace

Disparting me from Certitude, and
  fain
Would know the dream and vision
  ne'er again.
          Baruch Arnegriff.

It is said that in his last illness the poet Arnegriff was attended at different times by seven doctors

YOKE, *n.*
An implement, madam, to whose Latin name, *jugum*, we owe one of the most illuminating words in our language—a word that defines the matrimonial situation with precision, point and poignancy. A thousand apologies for withholding it.

YOUTH, *n.*
The Period of Possibility, when Archimedes finds a fulcrum, Cassandra has a following and seven cities compete for the honor of endowing a living Homer.

Youth is the true Saturnian Reign,
  the Golden Age on earth again,
when figs are grown on thistles, and
  pigs betailed with whistles and,
wearing silken bristles,
live ever in clover, and cows fly over,
  delivering milk at every door, and
  Justice never is heard to snore,
and every assassin is made a ghost
  and, howling, is cast into
  Baltimost!
          Polydore Smith.

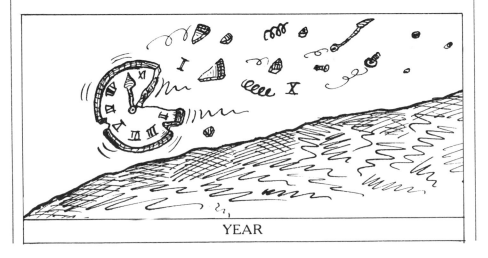

YEAR

Z

ZANY, *n.*
A popular character in old Italian plays, who imitated with ludicrous incompetence the *buffone*, or clown, and was therefore the ape of an ape; for the clown himself imitated the serious characters of the play. The zany was progenitor to the specialist in humor, as we to-day have the unhappiness to know him. In the zany we see an example of creation; in the humorist, of transmission. Another excellent specimen of the modern zany is the curate, who apes the rector, who apes the bishop, who apes the archbishop, who apes the devil.

ZANZIBARI, *n.*
An inhabitant of the Sultanate of Zanzibar, off the eastern coast of Africa. The Zanzibaris, a warlike people, are best known in this country through a threatening diplomatic incident that occurred a few years ago. The American consul at the capital occupied a dwelling that faced the sea, with a sandy beach between. Greatly to the scandal of this official's family, and against repeated remonstrances of the official himself, the people of the city persisted in using the beach for bathing. One day a woman came down to the edge of the water and was stooping to remove her attire (a pair of sandals) when the consul, incensed beyond restraint, fired a charge of bird-shot into the most conspicuous part of her person. Unfortunately for the existing *entente cordiale* between two great nations, she was the Sultana.

ZEAL, *n.*
A certain nervous disorder afflicting the young and inexperienced. A passion that goeth before a sprawl.

ZEAL

When Zeal sought Gratitude for his
    reward
He went away exclaiming: "O my
    Lord!"
"What do you want?" the Lord
    asked, bending down.
"An ointment for my cracked and
    bleeding crown."
           Jum Coople.

ZENITH, *n.*
A point in the heavens directly overhead to a standing man or a growing cabbage. A man in bed or a cabbage in the pot is not considered as having a zenith, though from this view of the matter there was once a considerable dissent among the learned, some holding that the posture of the body was immaterial. These were called Horizontalists, their opponents, Verticalists. The Horizontalist heresy was finally extinguished by Xanobus, the philosopher-king of Abara, a zealous Verticalist. Entering an assembly of

ZIGZAG

philosophers who were debating the matter, he cast a severed human head at the feet of his opponents and asked them to determine its zenith, explaining that its body was hanging by the heels outside. Observing that it was the head of their leader, the Horizontalists hastened to profess themselves converted to whatever opinion the Crown might be pleased to hold, and Horizontalism took its place among *fides defuncti.*

ZEUS, *n.*
The chief of Grecian gods, adored by the Romans as Jupiter and by the modern Americans as God, Gold, Mob and Dog. Some explorers who have touched upon the shores of America, and one who professes to have penetrated a considerable distance into the interior, have thought that these four names stand for as many distinct deities, but in his monumental work on Surviving Faiths, Frumpp insists that the natives are monotheists, each having no other god than himself, whom he worships under many sacred names.

ZIGZAG, *v. t.*
To move forward uncertainly, from side to side, as one carrying the white man's burden. (From *zed, z,* and *jag,* an Icelandic word of unknown meaning.)

> He zedjagged so uncomen wyde
> Thet non coude pas on eyder syde;
> So, to com saufly thruh, I been
> Constreynet for to doodge betwene.
> *Munwele.*

ZOOLOGY, *n.*
The science and history of the animal kingdom, including its king, the House Fly *(Musca maledicta.)* The father of Zoology was Aristotle, as is universally conceded, but the name of its mother has not come down to us. Two of the science's most illustrious expounders were Buffon and Oliver Goldsmith, from both of whom we learn *(L'Histoire générale des animaux* and *A History of Animated Nature)* that the domestic cow sheds its horns every two years.

ZOOLOGY

NOTE:
The Devil's Dictionary
appeared sometimes
on a regular basis
and sometimes at
long intervals in
weekly newspapers
around the country
from 1881 to 1906.
This illustrated
edition is abridged
from the edition
originally published
in 1911 by the Neale
Publishing Company.
That edition, and
many that followed,
comprised over 1,000
entries chosen among
the many more that
appeared during the
newspaper column's
25-year life.
Curiously enough, the
first publication in
book form of The
Devil's Dictionary
was entitled The
Cynic's Word Book. It
appeared in 1906, five
years before the next
one, and seven years
before Bierce's
disappearance and
presumed death in
Mexico.

The drawings in this
book are dedicated to
the memory of Ambrose
Bierce and to my
friends, Brad Holland,
Liz Thayer, Paul Fargis,
Hayward Cirker and
David Schneiderman.